To

[illegible]

My Best

[illegible]

Never to forget

April 20/02

A VOICE IN THE CHORUS

"I was moved by the pain and anguish [your book] contains. Like all survivors' testimonies, yours must be read by anyone committed to bear witness."

Elie Wiesel
Andrew W. Mellon Professor in the Humanities
Boston University

"Abraham Zuckerman's *A Voice in the Chorus* is a unique story, and at the same time, a universal lesson of life under duress. Abe Zuckerman has committed his story to writing so that future generations may read of one young man's struggle for survival in what was hell on earth in the Nazi era. Zuckerman's story teaches us that one can remain human throughout inhumane conditions if one's aim is survival and belief for a better tomorrow for our people and mankind."

Benjamin Meed
President
American Gathering of Jewish Holocaust Survivors

"The story of Abraham Zuckerman, a survivor of the Holocaust, must be required reading for every junior and senior high school student. The reader, young or old, will come to know of the attempted annihilation of a whole people simply because they were Jews.

"Woven throughout the story of this young man there is the story of moral courage to care on the part of the victims for one another; the courage to care on the part of those who risked their lies to save Jews.

"There is in this young man's account the story of 'the sanctification of life—*Kiddush Hahayim*' in spite of of the constant attempts by the Nazis to murder each one of God's people."

Rose Thering, O.P., Ph.D.
Executive Director
National Christian Leadership Conference for Israel

"It is important that your experiences be chronicled and available for history to record the truth about the events of that period."

Frank R. Lautenberg
U.S. Senator, New Jersey

"Abraham Zuckerman—truly a man for all seasons. He survived and succeeded through his courage and his intellect. His indomitable spirit serves as a shining beacon to us all. I am proud to be counted as a friend."

Jerome N. Waldor
Major General, U.S. Air Force

A VOICE IN THE CHORUS

Life as a Teenager in the Holocaust

Abraham Zuckerman

AMZ PUBLISHING

A VOICE IN THE CHORUS

First edition published 1991

Published by
A M Z Publishing
1325 Morris Avenue
Union, New Jersey 07083

Book design by Words & Deeds, Inc.

Printed in the United States of America

Library of Congress Cataloging-in-Publication Data

Zuckerman, Abraham, 1924–
A voice in the chorus : life as a teenager in the Holocaust / Abraham Zuckerman. — 1st ed.
p. cm.
1. Holocaust, Jewish (1939–1945)—Personal narratives.
2. Zuckerman, Abraham, 1924– . 3. Jewish children—Biography.
4. Holocaust survivors—Biography. I. Title.
D804.3.Z83 1990
940.53'18—dc20 90-30503
CIP

ISBN 0-962-7413-0-2

Contents

I dedicate this book to the memory of
my father, Wolf Josef, my mother, Anna,
and my sisters Hella and Dora,
all of whom were murdered by the Nazis

To my beloved wife, Millie
To my daughter Ann, and her husband, Bernard
To my daughter Ruth, and her husband, Steven
To my son Wayne, and his wife, Deborah Ann

To my grandchildren
Debbie and her husband Neil, Jeffrey, Jennifer,
Hillary, Michelle, Stephanie, Andrew and David
and my great-granddaughter, Julia
all of whom bring joy and happiness to my life.

To the martyrs and the survivors of the Holocaust
And to all those who will never forget.

A Personal Note

My purpose in writing this book is to describe my life as a boy in Cracow, Poland, the city where I was born, and to tell of my experiences during my youth, including the war years of 1939 to 1945. I was a witness to the horrors of the Holocaust and the near-total destruction of the Jewish community of my hometown. I have written what follows for my children and my grandchildren and for the generations to come in order to help perpetuate the memory of the tragedy of the Holocaust.

It has taken me many years, and much anguish, to find the courage to recollect these experiences and put them on paper. I hope that my words are adequate to express my feelings about the events I witnessed and the days and the years I lived through.

Abraham Zuckerman
Hillside, New Jersey

Heshvan, 5751
October, 1990

רַק הִשָּׁמֶר לְךָ
וּשְׁמֹר נַפְשְׁךָ מְאֹד
פֶּן־תִּשְׁכַּח אֶת־הַדְּבָרִים אֲשֶׁר־רָאוּ עֵינֶיךָ
וּפֶן־יָסוּרוּ מִלְּבָבְךָ
כֹּל יְמֵי חַיֶּיךָ

וְהוֹדַעְתָּם לְבָנֶיךָ וְלִבְנֵי בָנֶיךָ

Only guard yourself,
and guard your soul carefully,
lest you forget the things your eyes saw,
and lest these things depart your heart,
all the days of your life.

And you shall make them known to your children,
and to your children's children.

Deuteronomy 4:9

Acknowledgments

On May 29, 1949, the day that I arrived in my new homeland, the United States of America, I knew that this book would have to be written. Thirty-seven years later, after gathering the appropriate strength, courage and distance in time from the Holocaust, I began dictating my thoughts.

Many thanks to my cousin Michael Levin, who asked the questions which reawakened my memories and experiences. It was through his persistent questioning that I was able to remember so many important details.

Special thanks to my devoted secretary, Margaret Conroy, who, from the beginning of this writing, transcribed my thoughts onto paper.

To my son-in-law Steven W. Katz, who edited the final drafts and made numerous suggestions regarding this work, I cannot thank him enough.

To my wife, Millie, who had many sleepless nights as I relived the memories of the Holocaust, I thank her for her encouragement and support. Millie for forty-three years has been my partner in marriage, and I thank her for everything.

Introduction

This is a moving testimony to the horrible saga of the Holocaust as it is relived on these pages through the personal recollections and painful memories of a teenager. In his vivid description of the monstrous experiences he witnessed and was fortunate to survive, the author captures the many faces of this unconscionable and most terrible chapter in the history of mankind.

The arbitrary uprooting of whole communities from their homes of many centuries, the inhuman cruelty, the mass deportations, the random killings and the planned extinction of an entire people again come to life. But also the few rays of hope of truly righteous gentiles, both Germans and Poles, who often risked their own lives in order to save those of a handful of Jewish victims of this mad persecution.

At a time when the perennial detractors of the Jewish people again dare to cast doubts and even deny the very existence of the Holocaust, Abraham Zuckerman's narrative is an important contribution to our collective duty for posterity—to remember and never to forget so that such heinous crimes should never be allowed to happen again.

In his own words, "the Holocaust is impossible for people to thoroughly understand. So much hate, so much violence, so much pain, and so much death for so many years—who could possible grasp all this?"

It is for this reason that the outrageous events of this saga must be told and retold again and again.

Teddy Kollek
Mayor of Jerusalem

December, 1990

PART ❧ ONE

Cracow, Poland Before the War

Before I describe my own life, I should begin with some background about my family. My family consisted of my father, Wolf Josef, my mother, Chana, and my sisters, Hella and Dvorah. We lived in the city of Cracow, Poland, at Ulica Krakowska 24, or 24 Krakowska Street. My father was born in the town of Dukla, Poland. I don't know much about the town because he never really told me about growing up there. I traveled to Dukla once or twice with with my family when I was five or six. We went visiting during school vacation or during the Jewish holidays. My father's parents had seven children—five boys and two girls. They lived in different parts of Poland, except for two brothers, who lived in Kosice, which is now part of Czechoslovakia.

My father was a hat maker. My father's parents were also in the hat business, but on a much larger scale. My father made expensive fur hats, the type you wear in the winter. He made hats out of Persian fur. Most of his customers for the fur hats were wholesalers, people who had stores or stands in the markets. He also made less expensive hats for the general market. In addition, he made *straimlech,* the round hats that Eastern European Jews wore on *Shabbos,* on Jewish holidays, or at weddings or other special occasions. These hats were luxury items. My father's *streimel* business was unique in Cracow and his *straimlech* were in high demand. When people wanted *straimlech* made, the fur salesmen would recommend my father to do the work.

My father worked at home, in the kitchen. We did not have a very big apartment in Cracow, but the kitchen was large enough for him to set up shop there. My father's tools consisted of a sewing machine and his hands. Most of the work was done by hand. The *straimlech* were done entirely by hand. He would buy fur from a wholesaler. My father had some forms for the hats. Then the furs had to be sewn together and stretched, and then nailed and stretched again. It was a whole process to make a fur hat. I don't think he counted how many hours it took him to make each hat. He worked every day except *Shabbos* from morning until night, and that's how he earned his living. The hats were not cheap. As I said, fur was a luxury.

My mother was born in the town of Auschwitz, Poland. That was the German name. The Polish name was Oswiecim. My parents rarely spoke to me about when they were children. I only knew my parents the way young children know their parents. Because of the war, I didn't have the opportunity to grow up to adulthood and get to know my parents better. I was cheated of that experience. I was always busy going to *cheider,* religious school for young boys, until I was nine or ten, and then to *yeshiva,* religious school for older boys. So my time with my parents, unfortunately, was limited.

Like my father, my mother also came from a large family, seven girls and one boy. Auschwitz, where my mother grew up, was a larger city than Dukla. She told me that they had a happy life there, that it was a nice place to live. During the summers and *hol ha-moed* (the intermediate days of the Jewish festivals), we used to visit my grandparents. In Europe, *hol ha-moed* was family-

Above, Abe with his mother and sisters Dora and Hella in Europe before the war

Abe's grandfather, Elijakim Hornung, in Oswiecim

visiting time. Sucoth o Passover went on for eight days. This gave everybody a chance to visit each other. I also visited my mother's parents during vacation from school. During family vacations, I could enjoy myself and play with my cousins, who also came to visit.

My home in Cracow was a nice, warm home. We got along well. I was a middle child. My sister Hella was two years older than I. My other sister, Dora, was two years younger. Hella went to the *Bais Yaacov* school in Cracow, a famous school established by a woman named Surah Jenirer, a known leader in Jewish education. It was the first girls' religious school in Cracow. It followed the same format as a *Talmud Torah*, a traditional religious school for boys. At *Bais Yaacov*, the girls learned about the Jewish way of life—Jewish religion and Jewish customs. They learned to read, write, and speak in Hebrew and Yiddish. We were raised in a Jewish environment.

We lived in the *Kuzemark,* the Jewish section of the city of Cracow. The Kuzemark, which is known as Kazimierz in Polish, took its name from King Kazimierz Wielki (Casimir the Great) of Poland, who, in the fourteenth century, had invited the Jews to Poland to take part in commerce and trade. The *Kuzemark* was quite big—it wasn't just a few streets. Not all the Jews of Cracow lived in the *Kuzemark,* but most did. On *Shabbos* and on *yomtov*—the Jewish holidays—every store was closed. You could feel *Shabbos* and the holidays in the air. In the Kuzemark you could find everything that your heart desired. There were kosher butchers, kosher bakeries, Jewish grocers, Jewish book stores, large and small. Before the Jewish holidays, the Polish farmers would bring more of their goods into the markets in the Kuzemark, because they knew the Jewish people would be doing extra shopping.

There was commerce between the Jews and the Poles. In fact, rich Polish farmers would hire Jews to be their consultants in business. Some of them also hired Jews to manage their wealth.

Cracow today: part of the Krakowska Street neighborhood

Often, in the little villages, the Jew would serve as a broker to the rich Polish farmers. In Cracow, market days were twice a week. The farmers would bring their goods to the Cracow market. They brought vegetables, eggs, butter, and other farm products. With the money they earned from the sale of the produce, they would buy leather, textiles, farm machinery, all sorts of things, and all from the sale of what little they grew on their farms. The Polish farmers had a very good deal when the Jews were in Poland. The presence of the Jews enhanced the Poles' standard of living, through trade and commerce.

Not all the Jews of Cracow were wealthy and successful. Jews worked at every kind of job and trade. In Cracow there were Jewish shoemakers, shopkeepers, tradesmen, restaurant owners, everything. In those days, many Jews worked as *frachters*—package carriers between cities. This kind of business required young people. If you had a little business and you wanted something delivered right away—well, here, you call Federal Express. In Europe, you called upon a *frachter* to take the goods to another city, usually by rail or by horse and wagon. There were other people in the delivery business who were called *traigers,* and they had wagons that they pulled by hand and with a shoulder strap. They would line up at certain locations in the city. If anyone needed some merchandise sent to another store or to a wholesaler, he would hire a *traiger.*

Cracow was not just a commercial center. It was also one of the leading Jewish communities of Eastern Europe. There were many important synagogues in our neighborhood. There was the Alte Shul, the Hoiche Shul, the Cipper Shul, the Cyprus Shul, the Rav Isaac bar-Jekeles Shul, and many others. In addition, there was a Conservative temple. There were big synagogues and small *shteiblach,* neighborhood houses of prayer. Many famous rabbis lived in the *Kuzemark.* Everything was happening in Cracow. My father *davened* (prayed) in a number of different *shuls* (synagogues). During the week he davened in a *beis hamedrish,* which you could call a smaller, auxiliary synagogue, near our home. On *Shabbos,* we would go to other synagogues to pray.

Some Friday nights we went to the Alte Shiel, which was the great synagogue of Cracow. Today, unfortunately, it is a museum. It has Jewish artifacts—yarmulkes, Torah ornaments, and similar things. The sad fact is that there are not enough Jews left in Cracow to pray there. My father liked the cantor at the Alte Shul, so I went there with him some Friday nights. After the service, we would come home for Friday night dinner.

Sometimes, after dinner, we would go to the Tchechiover Rebbe or to the Melicer Rebbe, both of whom were important members of the rabbinate in Cracow. The program at their synagogues was called the *rebbe's tisch* (table). During the meal, the rabbi would speak about the *parashat ha-shavuah*—the weekly Torah portion. My father and I found it very interesting. In addition, a lot of the rabbis were great composers of songs. For instance, the Melicer Rebbe was an extremely accomplished composer. It was the greatest thrill for me to hear the Melicer Rebbe sing his *nigunim* (musical compositions). The synagogues would be so full that people would line up in the streets outside just to hear him singing.

On Saturday mornings, I davened with my father at the Mordeche Shaul's Bais Medrish. I was a *Belzer Chasid*—a follower of the *Belzer Rebbe*, a famous Chasidic leader. So, after the Shabbat meal, on Saturday afternoons I went to the Belzer *shteibel*. It was a ten minute walk from my home. I studied my *gemara*—my Talmud lessons there. I also studied the *sedra*—the weekly Torah portion there. My father was not a Chasid. He did not belong to any Chasidic following. He was a regular, gentleman Jew, but he did not stop me from being what I wanted to be. I became a Belzer Chasid because that is what most of my friends were. My friends studied at the Belzer shteibel, and I came to like the surroundings. As a matter of fact, my parents even sent me to the town of Belz to see the Rebbe himself. This was during the Shavuot holiday in the fall of 1939, just before the war began.

Anti-Semitism did not reveal itself in the part of the city where I lived. That part of Cracow was very religious. Our neighborhood was eighty or ninety percent Jewish. So you really didn't feel anti-Semitism there. If you went to the not-so-religious neighborhoods—of course, if you went with your chasidic outfit with the *pais,* the small sidecurls, you did not feel as comfortable. You could hear a slur sometimes—"Jews, go to Palestine!"—if you went outside the *Kuzemark*. You could also get pinched with a pin. Nobody was violent toward us, though. You could walk the streets at night without fear.

The Hoiche ("Tall") Synagogue on Juzefa Street

The Remuh Schul Synagogue on Szeroka Street, taken on a recent visit

Top: The Alte Shul Synagogue (Old Synagogue), also located on Szeroka Street. Taken on a recent visit with my wife and son.

Bottom: The Conservative temple

Isaac Bar Jekeles Shul Synagogue

I didn't have nearly as much contact with non-Jews and with nonreligious Jews as we have today. In those days, most of the Jews in the Kuzemark were religious. Today it seems unusual to some people if you *daven* three times a day. But back then, it wasn't something out of the ordinary. Almost everybody did it. You didn't have to be so very religious to go twice a day to the synagogue. This is the way people lived. When I was in school, we davened in school. When time came for davening, my father would leave everything and walk over to the synagogue to join the *minyan*, the quorum for prayer. Then he would come home again and go back to his work.

I loved learning Talmud and the rest of the Jewish curriculum. Most of us loved it. I started my studies at a young age. My parents put me into a private *cheider* (school).

Like everything else in the Jewish neighborhood of Cracow, the *cheider* was within walking distance of our apartment building. The rabbi, Yankel Landau, taught ten or fifteen children in his house. He was a famous *melamed* (teacher of children) in Cracow. Then, a year later, I "graduated" from his class and I went to another *cheider* for slightly older children. The *melamed* at that *cheider* was named Eli Schliefstein. A friend of mine named Abe Jachcel attended that *cheider* with me. He lived nearby. He now resides in America and is one of the very few people from this period in my life who survived the war.

A year after that, my father put me in the *Talmud Torah*, the Jewish elementary school. I was seven or eight years old. At the school, most of the children in the *Talmud Torah* were bright, and the reason was that we spent so much time studying Talmud.

I studied Talmud from five in the morning until nine at night, and I spent even more time studying on Shabbat. We were always studying, always learning Torah. There was not much time for playing with my friends. Some of my friends were sports-minded and they played ball. We used to make a ball out of old socks and old rags. At Chanukah time, and during certain other holidays during the year, we would learn at the Talmud Torah only half-day, and we spent the rest of the day playing games. Our life was mostly spent learning and learning, and I think it paid off.

I don't think I ever got in trouble as a child. The only problem would be if I didn't earn the top grades in class. But I never had that problem, so I cannot say what would have happened. Most of the boys were good, I suppose. We learned *gemara* from the beginning of the Talmud and straight on through. Sometimes when the holidays came around, we would study the

Talmudic tracts dealing with the specific holidays. The classroom had no central heating for the winter and no air conditioning in summer. We had wooden benches and wooden tables. The heat came from a coal-burning stove. It was primitive. We did not have the conveniences of today. But we liked it just the same. We did not know any different.

Our usual school outfit consisted of a long jacket, short pants, dark socks, and shoes without laces. In Cracow, we did not wear yarmulkes—we wore hats or caps. It was not the custom to wear yarmulkes in the street. Boys wore Chasidic-style

Talmud Torah (Hebrew School) on Estera Street where I spent most of my youth learning. This is a recent photograph.

caps. The caps had a very small visor and a soft or hard top. When you got older, you graduated to a hard top.

About the climate in Poland. The summers were nice, but the winters were very harsh. The winter started in October and didn't finish until Purim, which fell in March. The snow was very high and we used to walk, regardless of the weather. We put on our boots and we walked in the snow. During the summers, sometimes we would go to a resort in the country. My father would rent half a bungalow from the Polish owner. My mother, my sisters and I would stay there for part of the summer. My father would come only for the weekends. As I mentioned, we also went to my grandfather's for summer vacation for a couple of weeks. It was very enjoyable. We weren't rich. It was not easy to make a living and support a family in those days. All I did the rest of the year was spend my time learning Talmud. That was what I loved, anyway.

Here is a typical day from when I was growing up. I usually rose about five or six in the morning. My mother used to get up two hours before me. She wanted to light the stove and get a fire going so that the rest of the family would be warm and so that we would have fresh coffee for breakfast. To get the stove hot was not an easy job. You had to get special wood that burned quickly, and the fire always took a little time to get going, but that's a mother for you.

I also did things for my mother. I loved to do chores around the house and help out my parents wherever I could. I loved to do errands for my mother. On Thursday night, when the stores were open late, my mother would call on me to carry the shopping bags for her. The *Yiddishe Platz*, where we shopped, was a twenty minute walk from our house. We didn't have cars to take us places. It wasn't like it is here in America. There were no supermarkets. Instead, there were small stores in the marketplace, and you carried the bags home. You went to one store for a certain thing and to another for certain other things. There were

The Yiddishe Platz (Jewish Marketplace). The building in the background is where the butchers display their meats.

quite a few bags to carry, and it was a chore, but I was happy to do it to help my mother. It was part of *kibud av v'aim*—Hebrew for "honoring your father and mother."

Early in the morning, I would go first to the *Belzer stheibel*, the neighborhood house of learning, where we would "do *hazeres*"—which means that we would go over our studies from the day before. After studying, I would attend the minyan, or quorum of ten, for the morning service. Then I would go home for breakfast. Around nine, I would go to *Talmud Torah*, to school. At school we studied things long enough so that we could recite them by heart. Nothing was written. When you had a test, the answer had to be by heart. When you got the question, you answered from memory. After morning classes, if there was time, I would go home again for the noon meal. Then I would go back to school. In the afternoons, we would study the Polish curriculum every day for two hours. After that came recess and then we would go back to learning the Talmud until six or seven o'clock.

In the *Talmud Torah,* we were just like kids in any other school. There were *melamdim* (teachers) whom we liked and teachers we didn't like. *Melamdim* taught the lower grades. Teachers of higher grades were called *rebbes.* Some of the *melamdim* were angry individuals. There were thirty or forty *talmidim* (students) in a typical class. The *melamdim* were not especially likable people. It's not like here in America where the rabbi is your friend. The rabbis in Poland were strict, and we didn't like that.

Sometimes the students played tricks on the teachers they did not like in order to get even with them. Sometimes the students would mess up the rabbi's chair. They would take corks that you use in fake guns and put them in the doorjambs, where the rabbi couldn't see them. When the rabbi came in and slammed the door, the cork would pop. This would scare the rabbi, and it was the way for us to get even. The rabbis were always mad at us, always insulting us, but that was how things were then. Maybe that made us better students.

We would eat dinner in the afternoon, so I went home and we had a dinner at twelve or one o'clock. It was the other way around there—you had dinner at noon and a smaller meal later. After dinner, as I said, I went back to school. We studied the Polish curriculum, secular studies, from 1:30 to 3:30. The Polish curriculum included language, culture, history, science, current events—everything. I took the Polish curriculum seriously. It was not a burden for me to study these subjects. The usual program called for seven years of secular studies. The classes were interesting. The Polish-curriculum classes also met in the *Talmud Torah.* At the end of the seven years, we had to go to a public school to be tested on the Polish subjects and also to be graduated.

After the Polish curriculum, we had a break for the evening meal. I used to bring a sandwich from home to eat then. I would bring an apple and whatever else my mother prepared along with it. I would also bring a thermos bottle with coffee or milk. Then we would study until seven. I would go home again, and then I would go back to the *Belzer shteibel*, the neighborhood house of learning, and stay there until nine thirty or ten at night. The *shteibel* was a ten-minute walk from my home, maybe not even that far. This was how my time was usually spent.

The students were always very competitive—that is, the ones who wanted to make good grades were competitive. Some were competitive and some were not. But in those days, if you didn't make the grade, you didn't advance. You stayed back, and this was very embarrassing to your parents and to yourself. But this all depended on how you felt. Cracow was among the elite of Eastern European Jewish communities. Almost every boy got a full Jewish education, no matter how his parents felt about their *Yiddishkeit* (Jewishness). A father may or may not have prayed regularly or kept up with Jewish life, but he still wanted his children to be educated and to be knowledgable about Judaism. It seldom happened that a young person could come into a synagogue and feel strange about the environment. He would always know what was going on. Even as a boy, I felt that there was a certain flavor to the Jews of Cracow.

To educate one's children was very important to the Jews of Eastern Europe, just as it is here in the United States. Jewish parents believed that every child had to have a full education. It was difficult for most Jewish young people to be admitted to Polish universities because of anti-Semitism. For this reason, some young Jews would leave Poland to go to universities in foreign countries, and they would complete their education there. If the Nazis had not come to Poland, my parents probably would have wanted me to go to a university in a foreign country.

While I was attending the Talmud Torah, during late 1938 and 1939, Hitler deported all the Jews of Polish origin from Germany, and many of them came to Poland. A large number of them came to Cracow. When they arrived, they went to the *kahal*, the Jewish community center, for assistance. The *kahal*

was the Jewish city hall, and it was supported by the Jewish community. The *kahal* was a sort of social services agency, providing financial assistance to those who needed it. The *kahal* ran the schools—the Polish government did not support the Jewish schools. The *kahal* also took care of everyday life in the city. Marriages, divorces, *shochetim* (kosher butchers), *mashgiachs* (supervisors of kashruth), the *bais din* (Jewish court)—all these were functions of the *kahal.*

The *kahal* assigned the Jews coming from Germany to local families, and some of them stayed in our home with my family. The community reacted very humanely to the newcomers. Any Jewish family that had a decent apartment took them in. Some of the German Jews came with money, but many others had to get financial and moral support from the *kahal.* Some of the host families did not have enough spare beds, so some of the newcomers slept on the floor or two or three to a bed. I did not have much contact with them, even with the ones who stayed in our home. They would sleep in the apartment and then they would leave. We did not talk about life in Germany. I was too young to get into a conversation about that sort of thing. We took them in until they found a way to survive, or until they decided what they wanted to do with their lives. A lot of them left. A lot of them went to Palestine via different countries. They didn't wait for Hitler to come and kill them. Where they went after they left our home, I did not know.

1939: CRACOW, THE WAR BEGINS

WHEN THE WAR CAME TO POLAND, in September 1939, I was fourteen years old. We had air raids for the first two or three weeks of the war. The Nazis had begun to bomb the cities of Poland. We had to run into the basement of our apartment house whenever the alarms sounded and the bombing started. We had to darken the windows in the apartment. No one could drive a car at night with the headlights on. I realize now that it might not have been a good idea to go to the basement during the air raids, because if they bombed us from above, we might all have perished in the basement. Our landlord lived in the same apartment building. His name was Israel Schwartz and he had a tavern and a liquor store in the building. It was not a big apartment house—only nine or ten families lived there. The residents would gather in his store until the air raid ended.

The Polish government barely defended Poland from the Nazis. Although the Nazis did not bomb Cracow, they were responsible for a lot of sabotage. I think the Nazis caused this sabotage because they wanted to hamper Polish resistance to the war. For example, just before the war, as I remember it, a new bridge had been built a few streets from my home. They called it the Marshal Pilsudski Bridge, in honor of a military hero of Poland who was very supportive toward the Jews. The saboteurs mined the bridge and blew it up as part of their plan to weaken resistance to the Nazi invasion. The Poles witnessed events like the destruction of the bridge and they resigned themselves quickly to the arrival of the Nazis.

My family lived in fear—as did all the Jews of Cracow. Until September, 1939, the Jews of Poland were full citizens of Poland with all the rights and obligations of other citizens. There were even Jews in the Polish government. But we were very much afraid of the Nazis when they entered. The question of survival—the will to live and the need to save one's family—was uppermost in our minds now. As the war progressed, we became increasingly anxious. We saw Hitler's victories all over Europe. He had already entered Austria and Czechoslovakia, now he entered France, Holland, Belgium, and so on. It was a big shock for us to see him succeed so quickly. We feared we would no longer be a free people.

I graduated seventh grade before the war began. This meant that I was able to finish my secular studies before the Nazis entered Poland. I graduated with good grades, but unfortunately, because of the war, I could not continue either my secular or my Jewish studies. I attended Talmud Torah until the war started. After the war broke out, the Talmud Torah was closed.

I believe that the Nazis and not the Poles ordered the closing of the religious schools. In any event, the Jews simply abandoned the Talmud Torah out of concern for the lives of the children. We never knew what the Nazis' intentions were. Everything stopped. Parents were afraid to continue their children's education. However, so as not to abandon completely the education of the children, some of the rabbis held classes in their homes. My father paid the tuition for me to go to a rabbi's house to study. I went to the rabbi's house in such a way that I did not appear to be going to study. It would have been very dangerous for the students, and for the rabbi, if we had been caught. We would never carry books. Everything was left in the rabbi's home. We dressed like secular people—we did not wear our usual Chasidic outfits. We didn't dare. We had to go that way so that no one would recognize us as Jews. This shows you how important it was to my parents to continue their children's education.

The Nazis invaded Cracow about two weeks after the war began. After the Nazis came in, we were afraid to walk the streets. It was no longer safe for men or boys to be seen wearing *pais* (sidecurls) or anything else that publicly identified a person as a Jew. I saw the Nazis in the streets cutting the beards and *pais* of Jewish men, and I didn't want that to happen to me. The private classes in the rabbis' home only lasted about two months, and then I had to give these up, too.

Nazi soldiers cutting the beard and *pais* of a Jew in the street.

Life was completely different after the war began. There was a shortage of food. The Polish administrators, working under Nazi orders, started to ration the food. They distributed ration cards for bread and other essentials. My sisters and I had to stand in line at the bakery in the early hours of the morning to get bread. I think they gave two loaves to a person. We waited on line in shifts—I would wait two hours, and then my sisters would take my place, and so on, until the bakery opened. If you put your whole family on line and you had three kids there, you would get enough bread to make it through the week. I don't know whether the rationing was for everyone or just for the Jews. I think the rest of the population must have had some rationing. The officials also started to ration sugar, coffee, and all the basic food items.

From the very start of the Nazi occupation, conditions worsened for the Jews. We couldn't go to the yeshivas or the *shuls* anymore. We had to *daven* (pray) in private houses—in fear. Before the war, my father was able to earn a living, but I don't remember whether he could continue his business after the Nazis came. I think my father still had a few non-Jewish customers who bought fur hats from him. We had to worry about new rules and regulations that were announced almost every day, new actions by the Nazis. Suddenly we had to worry about surviving.

In the beginning, immediately after the Nazi occupation, I hid up in the attic with my father and the rest of the men in the apartment building where we lived. I remember that I used to stay in the attic and look through the round windows up there. I remember how the Nazis grabbed people and put them on their green open trucks. I can still see the trucks filled with the people who had been seized, and God knows what happened to them. We never heard of them returning. After a couple of days, though, we thought things might have quieted down, and we returned to our apartments. We thought things might be all right. We thought the period of seizing people on the streets was over for the time being, but we were wrong.

We did not know what the Nazis intended with all their new rules and regulations. We did not know whether they were deceiving us or telling the truth. They were still seizing people in the streets and taking them away. I always had to watch whenever I went into the street, to make sure the Nazis were not roaming around with their open trucks and vans. The minute I saw the open trucks, I would hide inside a building. They grabbed people and put them on the trucks, and the people disappeared. Some of the people who were taken away in this manner were from my immediate neighborhood.

Life was not normal at all. I don't know how my family survived that period of financial and emotional hardship. I guess we lived on whatever my father had saved. Jews were jailed in Cracow. Some were taken away to Auschwitz, where they were killed. Even at the beginning of the war, the Jews of Eastern Europe knew that the Nazis were throwing people into concentration camps and killing them there.

The Nazis began to commit atrocities almost as soon as they arrived in Cracow. The soldiers marched on to other cities, but the SS, the Nazi secret police, took over immediately. The SS increased the level of fear every day with all kinds of announcements. There was an announcement that you had to give up the furs that you had. So every little fur went to the Nazis. You even had to remove the fur collar from your coat, and the Nazis came to collect it. Then they came and looked in the attics. They conducted raids in the apartments and the houses. They used to go in and look for valuables, for gold and silver, for all kinds of valuables. The Jews of Cracow knew that these atrocities were not simply the acts of a few immoral soldiers. We knew that they represented the policy of the Nazi regime.

My family did not have too much in the way of jewelry or worldly goods. I remember I made a small hole in the wall for the

Abe's family's apartment house, Ulica Krakowska
No. 24, Cracow

little jewelry that my mother had. The walls were built of solid masonry. I drilled a hole and I put the jewelry in, and I cemented it, and I painted it back. We had little of value in the apartment. When the Nazis conducted their raids, word spread that they assaulted a lot of girls. From what I heard in my home, a lot of the women spoke of the assaults. The Nazis even looked in the bodies of the women, they even raised them to the table and looked inside them, to see if they had anything hidden, any diamonds or gold. As I understood it, the Nazi soldiers stole a lot of the valuables and sent them to their own families in Germany.

When the Nazis came into Cracow, and into each of the Polish cities, they took over the Jewish-owned enterprises. In order to do this, they would install a German as a *Treuhänder,* or custodian, for each of the Jewish-owned businesses. The custodian would learn the business. As he was learning the business, he would siphon away the inventory. The Germans then would force the owner to keep the business going until the custodian learned how to run it himself, and then they would liquidate the Jewish owner. As a result, many people lost their livelihoods and then they lost their lives.

During the latter part of 1939, the Nazis organized forced labor for the Jews. You had to have a kind of permit and stamps. Everyone had to have a certain number of stamps showing that he did his work. Everything went through the *kahal,* the Jewish community center I mentioned earlier. It was like a Jewish city

The *kahal,* the Jewish administration building, Cracow

hall in Cracow. The *kahal* was a go-between or negotiator between the Nazis and the Jews of Cracow. The Nazis would give orders to the *kahal,* and the *kahal,* under threat of death, was forced to carry out those orders.

One day, after a big snowstorm, the Nazis announced that the Jewish men would have to shovel snow. Most of the work that winter involved shoveling snow off the city streets or doing other jobs for the comfort of the Nazis. My father, like the rest of the men, had to do the shoveling. I substituted for my father, as I did not want him to have to shovel snow. They did not require boys my age to do the work. So I went there and worked for the day, and at the end of the day they gave me the stamp. If you had money, you could pay someone to substitute for you. He would get the stamp at the end of the day and give it to you, and you would pay him.

I substituted for my father. I would work, and at the end of the day I would get the stamp and give it to my father. I did not want him to suffer the humiliation of the physical labor. They did not allow you to substitute, but you did not tell them that you were doing this. The stamps were not handed out by the Nazis—it was done by the Jews in the *kahal.*

Everything was all right for the time being—as long as you had the stamp. This work involved about ten hours a day. I worked from eight in the morning until six or seven at night. That's what I had to do. At the same time, I had to take my turn in line at the bakery, waiting for bread. It was not easy to get up at two in the morning to wait in line when I had to be ready to shovel snow at eight a.m. These were hard times, but we thought it was all temporary and that the times would get better.

In addition to bread, we also had to stock up on potatoes. Even before the war, it was normal for large families to buy large quantities of potatoes. Winters were harsh and it was hard for farmers to bring their produce to the cities. Every fall, we would stock up on enough potatoes to last the winter. We would fill the basement in our apartment in Cracow because it was the coolest place to store food. Even before the war, we never wasted food. There was always something done with the leftovers. If there was stale bread, my mother would make a bread soup. We never threw out food. During the first winter of the war, even potatoes were not easy to find. Potatoes and flour was the menu for the wintertime of 1939–40. Potatoes kept our family full. The general population had access to meat and vegetables, but not the Jews. The others were not limited to bread and potatoes as were the Jews.

A lot of Jews ran away from Cracow, trying to escape the Nazi invasion and occupation of Poland. Many of them lost their lives in the process. A lot of Jews left Cracow and later returned sick and injured. They came back because they could not reach their destinations. The Nazis were moving faster than they were. My father considered the possibility of leaving Cracow and running away from the Nazis. After giving the matter a lot of thought, my father decided that remaining in Cracow for the time being would be best. He told the family that he had tried to flee during the First World War and it had not been the right move then. So he decided that we would stay in Cracow to see how the situation would develop.

I think that remaining in Cracow turned out to be a grave mistake. We should have left Poland for some safer country. If we had left Poland, we might have ended up in Russia or some other country, since we lived close to the borders of Czechoslovakia and Hungary. Maybe from there we could have gone further. I cannot tell you. At the beginning of the war, it was still possible to escape.

Life in Cracow was not going too well for my family or for the rest of the Jews of the city. Nevertheless, we thought we were going to bide the time, and suffer these inconveniences and disruptions, and that somehow, in time, life would return to normal. We hoped that somehow, at a later time, even with the war on, life might not be a hundred percent as it had been, but at least it would be bearable. As the war went on, though, the situation worsened. The Nazis continued to take away our rights, our pride, and our freedom. We could not practice our religion because the Nazis closed the synagogues and the Jewish schools. The Nazi occupation did not only affect our religious lives. For example, my father was not able to continue to conduct his business. He had to close his business because he could not get any more goods from his suppliers and his customers could no longer move around freely, as before. Also, we could not move around freely because we were afraid of the Nazis.

On the first of December, 1939, three months after the Nazi occupation began, the Nazis announced a new decree: all the Jews in the city had to wear armbands made of white cloth with a blue star of David. The whole Jewish population of Cracow, my family included, had to wear them. Then the Nazis also began to take the better apartments from the Jewish inhabitants. Jews had to leave their apartments and the Nazis stationed themselves in them. Every day, there was some new order or regulation to demoralize us. It was all done to weaken our spirit, to upset us, to make us lose our will to live. They committed these atrocities all the time. I remember the Nazis laughing as they committed their atrocities. It was fun for them.

All the Jewish institutions were closed down after the Nazis entered Cracow. The *Belzer shteibel*, where I did my studies, was no more. The *kahal* was still there because the Nazis required it to stay open. The members of the *kahal* could not dissolve the organization and the Nazis would not let them resign. Every time the Nazis needed Jews to work, they went to the *rosh hakehillah*, the leader of the *kahal*, and said, "If you don't deliver so many Jews, or do this, or do that, we will kill you all." Every order the Nazis gave came with the threat of death. Today, looking back, I know that people wonder whether members of the *kahal* were collaborating with the Nazis, perhaps in an attempt to save their own lives. This was not the case. I don't think that the Jews of Cracow were angry at the members of the *kahal.* There was no feeling that the Jews in the *kahal* were collaborating. Everyone knew they had no choice.

One day in April, 1940, there were announcements—leaflets in the streets and signs on the walls—saying that there was going to be a ghetto. All the Jews of Cracow would have to live there. There were ghettos in almost every city and small town in Poland. For example, there was the Warsaw Ghetto and the Lublin Ghetto, to mention a few, and now there would be the Plaszuw Ghetto in Cracow. This was the system the Nazis used to get all the Jews into one place. When the time came for the Nazis to liquidate the Jews, they would have them all in one spot, in the ghetto. Maybe that was the reason that the Nazis created ghettos for Jews. We were trying to survive and we lived in constant fear. No one knew what the next day would bring. Incidentally, to my knowledge, when the Nazis announced the ghetto for Cracow, all the educational facilities for the Jews ceased to exist.

My father resisted moving our family into the ghetto. I cannot describe firsthand living conditions inside the ghetto, because we did not go there to live. I know it was located at the site of the Orthodox Jewish cemetery in Plaszuw, a part of Cracow linked to the rest of the city by a bridge. The Nazis forced the Jews to build the streets of the ghetto with the tombstones from the Jewish cemetery.

I remember hearing, at the time, that the rav, or chief rabbi, of Cracow, Rav Kornitzer, and the leading Catholic priest of Cracow, whose name was Sapieha, went on a mission together. I believe that the mission was to Berlin. They sought to postpone the eviction of the Jews of Cracow from their homes to the ghetto. The rav and the priest went to the Nazi High Command in charge of Poland, to talk about the conditions in Cracow. They asked the Nazis not to move the Jews to the ghetto during the cold winter months, to wait for the spring instead. The Nazis deported the two religious leaders to Auschwitz, where both men were killed. I guess the Nazis didn't like that kind of interference. The Nazis sent their ashes back to Cracow. As I heard it, they even asked to get paid for shipping the ashes back to their homes. Well, our morale sunk lower and lower. For the Jews in Cracow, survival was the only thought on our minds.

Despite all of these atrocities, my father still would not leave Cracow. A lot of people had run away from Cracow before Hitler marched in. I don't know how far the people ran, but, as I said, many of them came back to Cracow injured or sick. My father said that he would not take his family away from Cracow because of his experience during the First World War. Dukla, my father's hometown, was in the war zone at one point during that war. He and his family were refugees, and the experience was very bad, so perhaps this explained why we did not leave Cracow at this point. We were children, of course, my sisters and I, and family life was very important. Our family in particular was very close-knit. You wouldn't dare leave your parents and run away by yourself. And they wouldn't send you away. That was Hitler's good luck, in a way, that the Jewish families kept themselves together. It was easier that way for the Nazis to capture us.

We were very worried when the Nazis marched into Cracow, but more than that, we were fooled. We took everything in stride—we did not know that the end would be that all the Jews were going to liquidation camps like Auschwitz to be put to death. That we didn't know, that we didn't expect. We heard stories about the other towns. We heard that in the other towns, the Nazis evicted the Jews from their homes, killed them, dismembered them. Somehow we did not want to believe it. We just did not want to believe it. How could that possibly be, we wondered.

As I mentioned, my father could no longer work as he did before. We had to live from the funds that he had saved. We couldn't go to *shul* or to school any longer, and that hurt us very much. When the High Holidays came, we had to *daven* in an apartment in our building and not in a synagogue. The apartment in which we prayed belonged to another Jewish family. One room of the apartment was located under the eaves of the building, directly under the roof. We assembled a *minyan* in that room. On Rosh Hashana and Yom Kippur, we went into that apartment. The people who lived there would move a tall chest of drawers in front of the door so that no one could tell that it hid a room. We would *daven* in that room. We were in danger, but we were determined Jews—we did our praying despite all the dangers.

Nothing was clear anymore, nothing was real anymore. We could never make plans from day to day because we did not know what would happen the next day. Every hour we heard all kinds of news. Anxiety swept over us. We did not know what to do. Confusion mounted. My father did not know whether to go to the ghetto or not. It is hard to say, and it may be wishful thinking on my part, but if we had moved there, perhaps other members of my family might have survived the entire ordeal of the Holocaust. My father took a trip to Dukla to see his parents, and to see how conditions were, but on his return, he decided not to move us there. Things were not as bad in Dukla as they were in Cracow, but my father could tell that that was just temporary.

I cannot describe exactly how it all felt. It was no good. I remember I felt trapped, endangered by what I saw going on, by the news I heard. But tomorrow, I hoped, was going to be a better day. I really hoped that things would change, that the war would end. We heard that the Allies in England and France had declared war against the Nazis. It gave us hope. We thought the war would end quickly as a result, but that was only wishful thinking. Nothing happened, it was just a big bluff.

The Poles gave away their country and the Nazis had a

smooth ride in capturing it. The French gave away their country and the Nazis had a smooth ride there. The Nazis were succeeding all over Europe, so it was really a tragedy for all the Jews. I was scared—my whole family was scared. I was very young when all this was happening. I did not know what was going to happen. My parents were worried about the children, about our home, and about every aspect of our lives. I wondered whether things would ever come back to normal. I wondered if the war would ever end.

CRACOW TO WIELICZKA AND BIALA-PODLASKA

THINGS WERE GETTING EVEN MORE FRIGHTENING. We finally had to move, to leave our home in Cracow. The event that triggered our departure was the announcement concerning the establishment of the Cracow Ghetto. As I said, during 1940, the Nazis announced that in March, 1941 we would have to leave our apartments and move into the ghetto. My father did not want to move into the ghetto. He was very fearful about the ghetto. Conditions in Cracow at the time became so frightening that we finally left the city. We took as much of the household goods as we could carry, and we abandoned our apartment with the remainder of our belongings.

We went to the next town, which was called Wieliczka, twenty or thirty kilometers from Cracow. I don't remember exactly how far it was. The town was known for its salt mines. We rented a room in a farmer's house and we stayed there for a while, with all our belongings piled up. As I think about it now, moving took half of our life at that time, because our personal possessions were so important to us. I think it was foolish to be so concerned about the personal possessions, because they only hindered our movement. When you have a family, I suppose you need all these items, so you have to take them with you somehow. We took what we needed most. The rest, including the furniture, unfortunately had to be abandoned.

We stayed at that farmer's house in Wieliczka for a while, and then the Nazis caught up with us. One day they chased us out and they put us on a train, just as we were—without any of our belongings. We were sent from Wieliczka to a Polish town called Biala-Podlaska. The town was situated not far from the Russian border and not far from Lublin, a larger Polish city. At the time, we did not know why we had been sent there. After the Nazis invaded Russia, I realized why they had sent us there. The Nazis sent us to this border town because they wanted to fill the town with Jews. They intended to use the Jews as cannon fodder, so that when the Nazis and Russians fired on each other, they would eliminate a certain number of Jews. I think this was the Nazis' intent—to have us killed in the cross-fire. Incidentally, when Hitler invaded Russia in June, 1941, we really thought that he was going to conquer the world.

In Biala-Podlaska, the Jews of the town took in one or two families each. We were obligated to work there for the Nazi administration. They put us to work cutting timber—chopping down trees and then cutting wood for the Nazi soldiers. Because of our work, they had wood for their stoves and heat. We also made mats from tree branches so that their tanks and their trucks could drive in the mud. We had to make thousands and thousands of feet of these mats. The sticks we used in the mats were made of tree branches three feet long and were tied with rope or some kind of wire. After we made the mats, they had to be rolled up and put on the trucks. The Nazis dropped the mats someplace near the Russian border so that when the snow came they would be able to continue their drive into Russian territory. We also cut wood for those trucks which used wood as fuel. These trucks had furnaces in the back, and they ran on a gas that was a by-product of the wood.

After a couple of weeks in this town, my father was very upset over what was happening to our family, and to the Jews as a whole. He saw that our situation was declining. He became very frustrated. He felt that we had no future in this town. As I remember him, my father did not look especially Jewish. He had a round, reddish face and he wore a moustache. One day, he put on farmers' clothing and took off his armband with the Jewish star. He took the train—illegally—to Dukla. He took an enormous risk. He was taking his life in his hands. It was hardly a life where we were, so he felt he had no alternative.

It was a long ride. The trip took nearly a day and a half to get first to Lublin and then from Lublin on to Dukla. He got there, somehow. He stayed with his parents, and he was very anxious to have us follow him. He tried, unsuccessfully, as it turned out, to get us passes so that we could travel legally by train.

On June 22, 1941, while my father was away trying to get us to Dukla, the Germans invaded Russia. A great deal of shooting, soldiers marching, and armor in motion accompanied the invasion. As I said, the house where we were staying was almost on the border. When the German army invaded, we were sleeping. It was during the middle of the night. The Nazis attacked the Russian fortifications no more than two or three kilometers from where we were staying. We were in a small, wooden two-room house. It literally shook from the cannon fire of the German bombardment. We lay on the floor of the little house, and the house was just shaking and shaking like it was made out of paper. It was a nightmare.

We were staying with a family that was also poor. The family consisted of a mother and her daughters. We were seven people crammed in that little house. As a result of all the bombing and shaking, I thought the house was going to cave in. If the house had fallen apart it would have killed us all, but what could we have done? Where could we have gone? Nobody can imagine how awful it was, waiting for the bombardment to stop. We were unbearably anxious—little children, my mother, my sisters, the other family, listening to the bombardment. Nobody can imagine how it felt to wait for it to end, but fortunately for us, the bombardment ended after a few hours.

After the firing ceased, we could see the Russian soldiers who had already been taken prisoners of war. We could see them marching. A lot of the Russians had been caught barefoot at the time the Nazis had captured them. The Nazis probably caught them sleeping—it was a surprise attack. I don't know what the Nazis did with their Russian prisoners. As for us, we were afraid to go out of the house. Whatever I saw was from the attic or the window slot. We tried not to be noticed. We learned the next day that the Russian fortifications contained a lot of food. The people from the town went to those fortifications and brought back food for us. We really needed that food because we had been going hungry for a few days. We had not been able to move, and we had run out of food in the house.

The Russian army was supposed to have some sort of fortress at that point on the border, some sort of impregnable fortress, like the French Maginot Line. From what I heard, though, the Nazis went right through it. The Nazis must have made use of spies. As I said, the purpose of sending us near the Russian border was that we would become victims of the war. Fortunately, though, this did not happen. Somehow, the Nazis moved deep into Russia on the first day. I was told that they went in approximately fifty kilometers, maybe more. The continued pounding and the bombardment that we had been expecting did not materialize. We owed our lives to the fact that the Nazis were so successful on the first day of the Russian invasion. If the fighting had continued on the border, where we were staying, we all most likely would have been killed.

If we had known what Hitler had intended for the Jews, we would have gone over the border from Poland to Czechoslovakia, and then into Russia, and we all might have survived. It was not legal to cross the Czech border, but there were plenty of places where we could have crossed. Why didn't we go? Again, it would not have been easy to travel with small children. And, of course, we didn't expect anything like the mass liquidations of the Jews.

A lot of Jews found themselves in Russia because Russia had occupied part of Poland. In that way, they were saved from Hitler. Russia saved hundreds of thousands of Jews, maybe more. True, they sent the Jews to Siberia, but they didn't kill them. The Jews might not have had much food in Russia then, but neither did the Russian people. In that sense, the Russians treated the Jews as equals. During the war, the Russians did the Jews a favor by sending them to Siberia. Back then, in Russia, the Jews were not killed. They were not tortured. They did not know what the Jews of Europe were going through. The Jews who had the good fortune to be in Russia survived.

As I said, my father was in Dukla when all this was happening. After a while, he sent us tickets so that we could join him. Or he might have sent us money to buy the tickets—I don't remember exactly. About a month after the Nazis invaded Russia, we took our chances. We removed our armbands with the Jewish stars and we traveled—my mother, my sisters, and myself—by night to Dukla. We were risking our lives. We were very frightened. We could have been shot if we had been discovered traveling without our armbands. I think we did not realize what could have happened to us. We really could have been killed for this daring voyage.

As far as I know, every town in Poland had Nazis and SS officers. There were soldiers, commanders, or officials in every town. My sisters wore babushkas and I put a big hat over my head and we went on the train, and nobody said anything. We were trying to dress like Poles. Of course, we had no belongings anymore, nothing. Somehow, we reached Dukla, and then we were all together as a family. My father had already rented an apartment, not much, two rooms in a house divided into four or five apartments, and we lived there for a while.

1941: Dukla

BY THE TIME MY SISTERS, MY MOTHER, AND I arrived in Dukla, the Nazis, not the Poles, were in charge. By now, incidentally, I was sixteen years old. The Nazis created a *Judenrat*, a governing body of Jews, even in little towns like Dukla, so they had a head of the Jewish community to whom they could give orders. The Nazis were actually in charge, but they forced Jews to be in the *Judenrat*. A lot of Jews did not want to take part because they feared that they would have to carry out inhumane orders. They did not want to be involved in it.

When I first arrived in Dukla I did not do anything but help with the house chores, but very quickly I had to get a job. All the Jews in the town were obligated to perform labor for the Nazis, and I was afraid that if I did not work, it could endanger my entire family. So, quickly, I had to get a job. In order to get a job, I had to notify the *Judenrat* that I was seeking work, so that they could assign me to some kind of work. I had to perform what they called "forced labor." Then I was assigned to a quarry on the outskirts of the town run by a firm called Emil Ludwig. All the company's work was performed solely by Jews, from Dukla and from the neighboring towns, who had been assigned there by the Nazis.

The Jewish workers mined the rocks and stones. I worked there for three or four months. I found it very hard. It was very hard work. My father tried to help me and make things easier for me because I was young and unaccustomed to that kind of hard labor. My father made contact with some individuals in town who had an "in" with the quarry company. He wanted to see whether it was possible to change my position at work. I wanted to work as an electrician. I had always dabbled a little bit with electricity and I thought I could pick up the work easily. The electricians had it easier than the people working at the quarry.

Some of the people who had contact with the quarry company were Jews. I guess my father paid them for their services. I do not know how much it cost for my father to get me that job. I didn't have to convince anyone that I knew about electricity. The individuals whom my father knew took care of it. They said I was an electrician. As I said, I was very handy, and I had no problem working in that department. I went to see them with my father, and somehow I was assigned to work in the electrical shop.

One of my coworkers in the electrical shop had a very similar background to mine. His parents came from the same towns as my parents, and his family had also moved from Cracow to Dukla. He had been assigned to the electrical shop before I arrived. His name was Jacob Fuhrer, or Yekel, as he was known to me, and we both worked as electricians. My friend Yekel was a little more knowledgeable about electricity than I was, so he taught me as we went along. I was very handy, so I learned quickly. We were called *Autoelektrikeren*—car electricians. My friend Yekel was also very handy, and he was very good to me.

My work at Emil Ludwig was divided as follows: I would work one week during the days in the shop as an *Autoelektriker,* and I would work the following week, at night, on the lighting. One of my duties was to take care of the lighting for the quarry, because the quarry was operational twenty-four hours a day. This meant that every night and every morning, I had to climb twenty-five-foot-high poles. In the evening, I would climb the

Yekel Fuhrer and Abe in 1946

poles with clamps attached to my shoes. I had to climb the poles and hang extremely large electrical lamps to shine on the quarry. The poles were located at the edge of the perimeter of the quarry. It was very dangerous work—the poles were thin and they swayed constantly in the wind. I was constantly afraid of falling, but I did the work because the alternative was going back to the quarry. I hung six or seven big reflector lights on the poles every night. In the morning, I had to remove these lamps and take them down to the storage area so that they would not be damaged when the workers were using dynamite in the quarry. At night, after I had hung all the reflectors, I would make the wiring connections for them. Then I had to go back to the machine room and start up a huge diesel generator. Somehow with my little body I managed to crank it up. It took enormous strength. It had a flywheel—a crank almost as big as I was. There were no automatic starters like today. Sometimes, I had problems—despite all my hard work, the generator would refuse to start. Some of the mechanics told me that if I poured a little gasoline on the carburetor, it would start faster. I wasn't allowed to do this, but it helped, and the generator would start right away. Hanging the lights was my night time job. During the day, I slept. I did all these tasks for a number of months.

I accepted this way of life—my family living in a small apartment, myself working at the quarry hanging lights and performing other duties. Somehow, my father was still working together with *his* father in the hat business, but they had to be secretive about this. By this time, the Nazis had restricted Jewish commerce and had forbidden us to run our own businesses. So the work had to be done in private. We managed to live because we were in a little town and we could trade secretly with the farmers for food and other necessities. We escaped the hunger and the abnormalities of life in Cracow and the other cities to which the Nazis had sent us.

One day, an order came down from the Nazis that all the Jews were to congregate at the church square in Dukla. Everyone went, with whatever belongings he or she could carry. The Nazis went from house to house, with whips and rubber truncheons, chasing people, making them move faster. One of the soldiers ran into our home and hit my mother over the head with a whip. She fell and fainted. Somehow, we revived her. My father and my sisters and I helped her out of the house to avoid more beatings.

We reached the square, where we found trucks waiting. It wasn't too far from where we lived. There, we were all lined up. They separated the younger people from the older ones. I

A recent photograph of Abe's grandfather's house, Dukla

remember that the Nazis' first action, while we stood in line, was to remove from the line those individuals who had reputations as community leaders. There were certain individuals about whom the Nazis were concerned. The Nazis thought these people might create some sort of disturbance, and the Nazis wanted to forestall any such actions.

Two groups of Nazis were involved in these events. The first group consisted of those Nazis who were stationed permanently in the town. The second group consisted of upper-echelon Nazis who came to Dukla to oversee the liquidation of the Jewish community and the deportation of the town's Jews. I could see the local Nazis discussing things with the newly arrived officers. The local Nazis pointed out the influential individuals in the Jewish community with whom they had dealt. The Nazis brought these individuals behind the church fence and shot them on the spot. The Nazis did this to stifle any opposition. They knew that without leaders we would never try to oppose them. I heard the shots.

At this point, the young men who, like myself, worked at the Emil Ludwig quarry were left alone. The others—the women, the children, and the older men—were loaded up on the trucks. All their belongings were left lying on the ground in the church square. I remember I wanted to go on the truck with my family. My mother pushed me away—she directed me not to come. She insisted that I stay with the other young men. When the trucks left, that was the last time I saw my mother, my father, or my sisters alive. I never heard from them or about them again. I missed them. I grieved for them. In one day, I became an all-around orphan, without any family, at the age of sixteen. To this day, I do not know where the trucks went with my parents, my sisters and the other people. They most likely ended up in Auschwitz.

A few years ago, I went back to Dukla to see if I could learn anything about what had happened to my family. At that time, I learned from the townspeople that the Nazis had brought Jews from Dukla to a forest outside the town in a place called Barwinek, near the Czech border. The Nazis shot the Jews to death and created a mass grave in the forest. I visited the forest with my wife. A local woman from the town of Dukla showed us the way to the gravesite in the forest. I have no way of knowing whether my parents and my sisters are there, in that mass grave.

After the trucks were gone, the Nazis ordered the rest of the young men who remained, myself included, to pile up the belongings in one corner of the church square. I don't know what happened to those belongings. Right after the trucks left, the Nazis took over part of the town and created a camp for the Emil Ludwig workers. That same day, only hours after the deportation of our families, they sent us back to work.

I was very broken up for a long time. I missed my family very badly. I felt devastated. I did a lot of crying, almost every day for quite a while. I did not want to believe what had happened to my family. I thought that perhaps someday I would see them again.

Gravestone, forest near Barwinek, where the Nazis slaughtered the whole population of Dukla.

Inscription on gravestone at the mass grave of the Jews from Dukla reads:

Here in [this mass] grave
lie over 500 Jews from
Dukla and Rymanow
who [perished in] a martyr's death
at the hands of German murderers.
August 13, 1942

Somehow, this hope kept me going. In the end, the hope was to no avail. After the war, no one came back. For myself, though, hope was the key to my survival. I made a conscious decision to do everything in my power to survive because I hoped I would see my parents and sisters again. Although my hopes were dashed in the end, they kept me alive throughout the ordeal of the war. I kept hoping and hoping.

☆ ☆ ☆

After the liquidation of my family, I was assigned new living quarters. My living conditions were extremely unpleasant. I found it very hard to get used to the meals they served. First of all, the food was *traife* (non-kosher). What they fed us tasted horrible. I barely ate at all. The food was made from potato peels, and it was covered with some kind of grease. It was really inedible. But you can only go so many days without eating, so I had to start feeding myself. I forced myself to eat what they gave us. Our diet consisted almost entirely of potato peels. That was the most you could get to nourish yourself. There was a Yiddish song about eating *bulves* (potatoes) every day. That became the literal truth in the camp at Dukla.

At night, everyone had to make a bed for himself. They did not provide us with beds or mattresses. I had to put some boards next to each other, and I would sleep on them. But that was all there was. As for the clothing that I had—it was still the same that I had been wearing the day I left home. That's all I had. That's all I owned. I had one shirt and I kept washing it and drying it at night so I could wear it in the morning. We were very seldom able to bathe. I just tried to wash up somehow.

The day after we were assigned our quarters, I was sent to work during the daytime in the garage at Emil Ludwig. I had to repair and shine the motorcycles of the Nazi soldiers. The Nazis would come in riding motorcycles, saying, "This doesn't work," "That doesn't work." Somehow we fixed the motorcycles. Whether we fixed them for long I don't know, but I polished them up and I fixed them, and the Nazis would go on their way. I was always relieved when they left.

The Nazi soldiers with the motorcycles were mostly young, although a few were middle-aged. They knew that we were Jewish, but they related to us primarily as mechanics. I thought of them as Nazis, and I was afraid of them. I sometimes wondered if a Nazi who had come in with a motorcycle was going to kill me. I could never be sure that I was satisfying them. I was afraid that one might slap me if I didn't do the right thing.

Most of the time, though, we would do no work at all. I would watch through the window to see whether anyone was coming in. If we saw someone coming, we would make ourselves busy. My friend Yekel and I worked in the garage with another person our age, a Polish fellow. He was very nice. He sometimes brought us bread because he knew how badly we were fed. Through all this time, from the day my parents and sisters were taken away from me, I never stopped thinking about my family—about where they were and what had happened to them. I grieved all the time. All kinds of rumors went around. Everyone talked about it because everyone's family had been taken away. The rumors said that everyone had been killed not far from Dukla, or, alternatively, that everyone had been taken to Auschwitz. I did not want to accept any of this. I continued to hope.

You might wonder how a yeshiva student learned to do electrical and mechanical work, how I learned to climb poles, attend to generators, hang lights in a quarry, and repair motorcycles to the satisfaction of Nazi soldiers. I learned the electrician's trade because I was always a handy person. I could pick things up just by watching people. Just by looking, I could tell how to do something. I did not learn about these things in *cheider.* In school we studied other subjects, not trades. I just came by the knowledge myself.

The German truck drivers would also come to the maintenance garage when they had problems with their trucks. The batteries needed to be repaired or overhauled. Sometimes we would make one battery out of two old ones. The batteries were extremely heavy—they took at least two people to carry. They were about two feet by three feet in size. They did not look like car batteries of today. The box that contained the battery was made of wood. The battery itself was made of lead plates connected together. The plates often needed to be repaired or replaced. We didn't have any new ones, so we had to dismantle old batteries and use the parts. I would replace the battery acid, mold the corks with a mudlike clay, and then recharge the battery and put it back in the truck. I also fixed the trucks' lights, the ignition systems, the starters—whatever needed fixing. I did the best I could, and I missed my family.

At Dukla: Fritz Zachmann

ONE OF THE DRIVERS WHO WORKED FOR the Emil Ludwig quarry company, trucking the stones up from the quarry, took a liking to my friend Yekel and me. He was a wonderful man named Fritz Zachmann, an older gentleman. We were kids compared to him. We were in our teens and he must have been in his fifties. We made his acquaintance one day when he brought his truck to the shop with some kind of problem. He did not wear a uniform—he was just a driver. He felt compassion for us. He took a liking to us and came to visit us in the maintenance garage. He visited us almost every day.

At Dukla, Mr. Zachmann saw the deportations and the atrocities that went on. He would tell us what the Nazis were doing to the Jews, and what they were planning, and as well as how the war was going. I could tell that he did not care for what the Nazis were doing, in Dukla and everywhere else. We found it extraordinary that under these circumstances someone would speak to us so critically about the Nazis. We could tell that he did not like what was going on. He did not like it at all. I remember that Mr. Zachmann gave me his address. I made myself remember it throughout my time in the camps. I promised myself that after the war, if I lived through it, I would visit him.

My strongest memory of Fritz Zachmann is from several nights after the deportation of the Jews of Dukla. I felt I could trust him, so I asked him if he would take me back to the house where my family had lived. I didn't have any clothes with me other than what I was wearing, and I wanted to get some more clothing. He agreed to drive me over in his truck. He took a chance by doing this. He ran an enormous risk, but it did not seem to concern him much. He did it, I suppose, because he thought it was the right thing to do. He was violating the rules by taking a prisoner out of the camps. If we had been stopped, we both would have been severely reprimanded or punished. We could have been killed for what we were doing.

That night, he drove me in his truck. When we reached the house, I was hesitant and afraid to enter because the house was empty—it was so strange to go back to the place where I had last lived together with my family. I summoned my courage and Mr. Zachmann and I went inside. Everything my family owned was still intact. It was all just lying there. I took a lot of the cut material my father had left, fur that he had cut out for hats. I also found some addresses of my father's Polish customers. I took whatever I could, as well as some clothing for myself. Whatever I could not use I gave to Mr. Zachmann. I gave him our silver candleholders and silver cups. I gave him the silver because otherwise it would have been stolen or taken by other people. I did not want to leave it there. I thought it much better that Mr. Zachmann should have these items—I did not want to abandon them to strangers, or to the Nazis.

I knew, as I was riding with Mr. Zachmann, that I could have run away—that I did not have to return to the camp. No one would have blamed him, because no one expected German truck drivers to be taking Jewish prisoners for rides. I did not run away, though. I went back to the camp. It was a very hard

Fritz Zachmann, 1946. Righteous among the Gentiles.

decision to make. I had no place to run. I had no family, as far as I knew. No relatives. Where was I supposed to run?

We returned to the maintenance garage and I hid the fur there. Later, I packed it all up. I asked Mr. Zachmann to send it away for me to my father's customers and to put his return address on the parcels. My father had been making hats for these people at the time of the deportation. As a result, I was able to receive money from them, through Mr. Zachmann. They sent the money to Mr. Zachmann, and he passed it on to me. These Polish people had been my father's customers for years. The money they sent came in handy later on. In Dukla and in Reichshof, where I went next, if you had money, you could buy some extra food from people who had connections to the Polish people outside the camp. The people outside the camp would somehow smuggle food into the camps. With the money that came in from my father's customers, I was able to buy myself some extra food.

It was fascinating to me that Mr. Zachmann and I developed a friendship. He was a wonderful man. Only lately have I begun to realize just how dangerous it was for him to take me out of the camp. He put his life on the line for me. Even when I was liberated, I still did not appreciate the magnitude of his courage. Now, many years later, I understand how brave he was. For me, he is one of the people the Jewish tradition calls the *hasidei umot haolam*—the righteous Gentiles of the world.

1941: Reichshof/ Rzeszow

DURING THE SUMMER OF 1941—to be honest, I did not know what month it was—I was moved by train from Dukla to the town of Reichshof, or Rzeszow in Polish. I did not know why we were leaving Dukla, but they cleared out the entire camp. It seemed like a spur-of-the-moment decision on the Nazis' part to move us. I remember I arrived at night and that we were put in houses. We lived in houses that had been part of the Jewish ghetto of Reichshof. Earlier, the Nazis had turned the area into a closed Jewish ghetto and then they had liquidated the Jews who lived there. Then they converted it into a sort of camp. The houses were empty, so they made them into a labor camp. It was not really a concentration camp or a death camp—it was just an encircled section of the town, regular homes that the Jews had inhabited before their deportation. Reichshof was just a camp for the purposes of gathering Jews for transit.

I slept in a three-level wooden bunk bed. We called the beds *pritches*. Jewish prisoners must have been there before us because the beds were already in the rooms when we arrived. The beds looked as though they had been used not long before. We slept ten or twelve to a room. The bunk beds had no bedding. Instead of a mattress I had a burlap sack filled with straw. I had blankets but no sheets. I slept on the burlap. The toilets were communal. I was not forced to do any hard work. I spent most of the time sitting and waiting, trying to avoid any commotion or pushing and shoving. I always stayed on the sidelines, and I was always on the look-out. That was always very important for me, to remain aware. Whenever there was commotion, there were fatalities. Staying alive and not getting hurt was my aim.

There were certainly deaths in Reichshof. By this time I knew—we all knew—that the Nazis were killing the Jews. My parents and sisters had been taken away, and I still had not gotten over that. I knew they hadn't just gone voluntarily. And they must have suffered horribly. That hurt me awfully. It was always on my mind. I continued to grieve. And I can imagine how my mother must have grieved about me. Had she still been alive, that is.

At Reichshof, the Nazis roamed the camp with dogs. They had big dalmatians. The Nazis loved their dogs. They trained the dogs to chase the prisoners. The Nazis never needed a provocation to attack people with dogs or even to shoot people. They shot on sight and at random. We could never disobey orders. The atmosphere among the Jews there was always one of fear. I was afraid. I didn't see any courage there. I did not expect to survive. I thought it was all going to come to an end soon. This was still the beginning of the ordeal, in many ways. I did not realize how much worse it could get. I thought this was the worst. I was afraid of being killed at any moment. The Nazis came around with their dogs and we had to hide wherever we could.

One day, the Nazis decided to liquidate the Jews who were in Reichshof. We were to be rounded up and taken to an assembly point. I don't know what gave me the idea, but I decided not to go. I knew that whenever they moved you, bad things happened. They might take you straight to the crematorium or torture you or shoot you. In Reichshof I certainly saw atrocities, but I thought I could somehow avoid them there. The Nazi policy was that when they took you to a new place, you did not know what to expect.

When they ordered us to assemble that time, I hid under the bed. I covered myself with a blanket. There was no one else in the room, no one in the building. The Jewish policemen were ordered to go around and see if any people were left. The Nazis used Jews as policemen over other Jews. The Jewish policemen were supposed to chase the rest of the Jews to the assembly place. Somehow this one policeman saw me. I didn't know who he was, but I knew he was Jewish. I stuck my head out a little bit from the blanket, and he said, "Come on!"

I told him in Yiddish, "Go away, make believe you didn't find me. Forget about me. Make believe you didn't see me." And he laughed. Fortunately, he listened to me. He must have been a nice person. I remained there, and I survived—at least until the next ordeal. Everyone else in my room was sent away. A few others from the other houses also remained. There was no specific accounting as to which of the Jews were sent away and which ones stayed in Reichshof, so I was able to be with the others who stayed. And now I was all alone—I had no remaining relatives. I was just seventeen years old and I was very, very frightened. Somehow I managed to stay alive in Reichshof.

I didn't know at the time what happened to the prisoners who had been rounded up, but I assumed that wherever they went, I would be better off staying in Reichshof. My reprieve did not last long. Not long afterwards, the Nazis liquidated the remaining Jews in the Reichshof camp, so there was no alternative—I had to leave. Hiding under the blanket that time was the right move on my part because I heard later that all the other people had been sent to Auschwitz.

SPRING, 1942: PLASZUW

WHEN I WAS REMOVED FROM REICHSHOF CAMP, I did not know where I was being taken. The conditions of the trips from one camp to another were never too good. We were taken from Reichshof camp in open cattle cars. It was a short trip—only a couple of hours, as I remember. We were moved to Plaszuw, a town across the Visla River from Cracow. My friend Yekel Fuhrer and I were sent to a labor camp there called Julag, the abbreviation for *Judenlager,* which meant "camp for Jews." At Julag, there were wooden barracks for us and we again slept in bunk beds called *pritches.* Ukrainians in black or green uniforms manned the camp and the guard towers around the barracks.

When I arrived in Julag, they assembled us for a head count. They also demanded to know what trades we knew. Whenever I was assigned to a new camp, I always told them I was an electrician. My friend Yekel was also listed as an electrician. They assigned us both to work for a company called Ostbahn. They mostly did repair work on trucks and cars. The fact that I told them I was an electrician saved me from hard labor—it was a lot easier to work on trucks than to perform hard labor. I worked ten hours a day, six days a week in Julag. I don't know what the other people were doing, but Yekel and I were assigned to the repair shop. I did electrical work on trucks, replaced the starters, fixed batteries, and fixed the wiring. That was the kind of work I did at Ostbahn. We went to work from the camp by truck.

While I was in Julag, I contracted typhus. The disease is highly contagious. Many of the prisoners came down with it. A lot of them did not survive. I don't know how I contracted it. Malnutrition and unsanitary conditions were most likely to blame. It is a terrible sickness. When I became ill with typhus, I couldn't walk. It makes you weak. Your limbs and your muscles get so weak that you can't stand on your feet. Your feet don't hold you. I literally became immobile, but I was afraid to stay in the barracks or to go to the infirmary. That would have been the end of me. All I had to do was tell the kapos—the prisoners the Nazis used to guard us—that I was sick and they would have shot me right away.

I did not go to the infirmary, because if you went to the infirmary it was an absolute certainty that you would be killed. If you were sick, you could not work, and if you could not work, you were of no use to the Nazis. So the kapos who worked as orderlies in the infirmary killed anyone who came in for medical attention. Or the Nazis themselves would take the people who went to the infirmary and shoot them and deliver them straight to the crematorium. This being the case, I went to work despite the typhus.

My friend Yekel stood next to me, and he held me up when we were marching. He helped me walk. He did it in such a way that the guard would not notice. Once we arrived at the shop, we would be assigned a particular vehicle to repair. I would go into the cab of the truck and I would lie down there for the whole day. Yekel was covering up for me and looking out for me, so that the foreman would not notice that I was lying inside. Yekel watched out for the Nazi soldiers and officers, too. Whenever they came around, he would alert me to their arrival. Despite my illness, I would pretend to be working in the cab. In a few days I felt better and I regained a little of my strength. I recovered from

The Polish government's Holocaust memorial at the site of the Plaszuw Camp, which makes no mention of Jews. The inscription on the memorial is translated from Polish as follows:

In Homage
To the martyrs slaughtered
by Hitler's genocide hordes
in the years 1943–1945

דינקום נקמת דם השפוך
TU NA TYM MIEJSCU SKATOWANO, WYMORDOWANO
SPOPIELONO W LATACH 1943–1945
KILKADZIESIĄT TYSIĘCY ŻYDÓW
SPĘDZONYCH Z POLSKI I WĘGIER.
NIE ZNAMY NAZWISK POMORDOWANYCH.
ZASTĄPIMY JE JEDNYM SŁOWEM
ŻYDZI
TU NA TYM MIEJSCU DOKONANO
JEDNEJ Z NAJSTRASZLIWSZYCH ZBRODNI.
MOWA LUDZKA NIE ZNA SŁÓW NA OKREŚLENIE OHYDY TEJ ZBRODNI,
NIESAMOWITEGO BESTIALSTWA BEZWZGLĘDNOŚCI I OKRUCIENSTWA
ZASTĄPIMY JE JEDNYM SŁOWEM
HITLERYZM
PAMIĘCI POMORDOWANYCH
KTÓRYCH OSTATNIM KRZYKIEM ROZPACZY JEST
CISZA TEGO PŁASZOWSKIEGO CMENTARZA
SKŁADAJĄ HOŁD OCALENI
Z FASZYSTOWSKIEGO POGROMU
ŻYDZI.
ת.נ.צ.ב.ה

Opposite: Plaszuw: the Jewish community's memorial to its martyred dead at the Plaszuw camp. The inscription on the memorial, translated from the Polish, is as follows:

In this place the torment, slaughter and the turning into ashes of tens of thousands of Jews from Poland and Hungary took place from 1943 to 1945. We do not know the names of the slaughtered. We substitute these names with one word

— J E W S —

Here was perpetrated the most horrible of crimes. Human language contains no words to describe the horror of this crime against humanity, its indescribable bestiality, despotism and cruelty.

We substitute these atrocities with one word

— H I T L E R I S M —

To the memory of the slaughtered whose last cry of despair is the silence of this Plaszuw cemetery. Homage is rendered here by the survivors of the Fascist slaughter.

THE JEWS

the typhus naturally—without any treatment. Somehow, I got better.

The name of the commandant at Julag camp was Miller, and he was an unusually vicious person, even by Nazi standards. A lot of killings went on in Julag. A lot of people perished in that camp. It was an extermination camp. They even brought people from other places to be killed there. Julag was the first place where I saw people shot right before my eyes. I saw this happen almost every day. I saw all kinds of atrocities. It was the first place where I saw people being killed on a regular basis. I really began to see the result of this horrible war.

In Julag camp I also met a first cousin of mine on my mother's side, a man named Maximilian Hornung. He was much older than I. He had been a very wealthy lawyer before the war. We were in Julag together for roughly the same amount of time. I would see him again after the war, but, of course, I did not know that at the time.

The food in Julag camp was very meager. I was so very undernourished and overworked. The traveling to and from work wore me out. In addition, I always had nightmares in the camps. What I saw in the camps was so horrible and unbelievable that I had nightmares about it. I had nightmares about my home. I had nightmares about my parents and sisters. I thought, "Where are my parents now?" I never wanted to believe they were gone. To this day, it does not seem possible. To this day, my mind still cannot accept the fact that they were killed at the hands of the Nazis. I always had nightmares about what was going on in the camp. As for survival, I took things day by day. I didn't consciously *think* about survival, but I *fought* for it. I always hoped that someday the war would end, and that when it ended, perhaps I would find some members of my family. Unfortunately, I did not find anybody after the war.

Remnants of the wall of the Plaszuw camp

WINTER, 1942: PLASZUW CAMP

LESS THAN A YEAR AFTER MY ARRIVAL IN JULAG, I was moved again, to another concentration camp. I was still about seventeen years old. This time it was the camp in Plaszuw, itself not far from Julag. At Plaszuw, they did not ask me my profession. There I was assigned to work in the coalyard. I was loading and unloading trucks of coal. It was horrible work, handling coal, because of the dust. You would get the dust through your whole body. It went through your nostrils. It went through your eyes, through your ears.

In Plaszuw camp, the Nazis ordered everyone to be tattooed. They tattooed me on my left wrist, on the place where you wear a watch. The tattoo said *KL,* which stood for *Konzentrationslager,* German for "concentration camp." The doctor who tattooed me did not do a good job. He was an old man. Over the years, my tattoo wore off. The living conditions in Plaszuw were the same as in Julag. I slept in a barrack. They gave me a *pritch* (bunk bed), and that's about all. I had to go out to the camp kitchen and see what I could get in food. I used to go to the kitchen with my *menashke,* a soldier's pot or pail.

In Plaszhuw, to my surprise, when I went to the kitchen for

my food, I encountered my childhood friend Moniek Pantirer. Until then, we had not seen each other since our separation after the Nazis moved into Cracow. I had a lot of friends when I was growing up in Cracow. A few of them are still alive today, but most perished in the camps. I don't know where they ended up. Moniek, or Murray, as he is called today, and I studied together as young boys in the Talmud Torah in Cracow. We were in the same class and we also lived around the corner from each other in Cracow. He lived at Ulica Juzefa 16 and I lived at Ulica Krakowska 24. He came from a large family, but unfortunately, no one else in either of our families survived.

When we were young boys, Moniek and I met in Cracow in *cheider* (religious school). When the war started, we were separated. Each of us did not know what was happening to the other. When I was transported to Plaszuw camp, I was very hungry and I was looking for some food. I happened to go into the kitchen, and there I found my friend Moniek, who was working there. We rekindled our friendship in the concentration camp at Plaszuw. It was fortunate for me that my friend Moniek worked in the kitchen there. Sometimes I would sneak into the kitchen and give him my *menashke,* and he would fill it with soup. I would return to my barrack with the food and I would eat it up, and that would hold me for a while, because, in the camps, the food we got was never enough. Sneaking into the kitchen this way to get more food was not dangerous. There were so many thousands of people at this camp that I was not really placing myself in danger by getting some extra food.

The camp at Plaszuw was like a little city. The Nazis used Jews as policemen and they even made one Jew the chief of police. The policemen were called "O.D. men," which stood for *Ordnungsdienst*—"order duty." Their job was to maintain order. Some of the Jewish policemen were willingly collaborating with the Nazis, and they abused and harassed prisoners, to better their own situations. However, some of the Jews who worked as

Abe and Moniek in the Displaced Persons Camp, Bindermichel, 1946

policemen did so against their own will. In the end, collaborating did not help them. One day, the Nazi commander of the camp, whose name was Amon Goeth, ordered them all out of their quarters and shot them all in the yard of the camp. He did so on the pretext that they were going to run away from the camp. So collaborating with the Nazis didn't save anyone. After liberation, some of the O.D. men were caught, tried by various governments, convicted, and hanged for collaborating with the Nazis and torturing and abusing the prisoners.

One day in Plaszuw—it was on Yom Kippur day, the Day of Atonement, the holiest day in the Jewish calendar—we heard that a couple of women had run away from the camp. As punishment, the camp commanders ordered the Jewish police-

men to round up several hundred of the prisoners, myself included. We were ordered to march up a hill in the camp where most of the shootings took place. We prisoners called this hill *Hujowa Gorka.* This was the prisoners' name for it. Translated into English, the name of the hill is not a printable expression. The name symbolized our resignation to the idea that we had no control over our own destiny. The hill was famous because they shot prisoners there and the bodies just fell over the cliff. And on Yom Kippur they took me up there, along with several hundred other prisoners.

I can tell you that I was not afraid. I did not think much about it. I thought to myself, "If this is the end, it's the end." We were left to stand there for quite a while. To my surprise, they did not execute the order to kill us. Instead, somehow, the Jewish chief of police, whose name was Chilewicz, gave us a lecture. He hollered at us on account of the two women who had run away from the camp. I think he had some compassion for us and he only put on a display of anger for his Nazi superiors. Finally, at the end, he said, "Go back to work." He sent us back to work, so we were not punished on account of the people who ran away. I think he gave us the lecture in order to appease the Nazis. This somehow saved us from being killed.

One might ask whether my attitude toward God changed as a result of seeing all these horrible atrocities. This is a very delicate question. It's very hard to give an answer. I think you have your answer when you see all the atrocities, when you see all the killings, when you see all the little children being killed. One night, for example, in Julag, as I slept in my barrack, they brought in twenty-two women. I don't know where the women came from. I think that Nazi soldiers discovered them in hiding, arrested them, and then brought them to our camp. In any event, the Nazis brought the women into the back of the barrack, which happened to be where my bunk, or *pritch,* was located. My barrack was located at the edge of the camp, next to the forest.

Nazi commander Amon Goeth riding a white horse outside of Plaszuw while the killing goes on inside the camp.

The Nazis just shot all of them with dumdum bullets right in front of our eyes. Dumdum bullets explode on contact with a human body. It is a very brutal way of killing. In the morning, flesh was all over the ground of the barrack. So, when you ask, did my attitude toward God change—what do you think the answer is?

PART TWO

Herr Oskar Schindler: February, 1943

ONE MORNING, WHILE I WAS IN THE concentration camp at Plaszuw, a number of us were called out from the barracks to the *Appelplatz*—the assembly square. I was scared when this happened. I didn't know why we had been called out or why I had been included, but I was very tired from my work in the coalyard. I figured, whatever happens to me will happen, because I could no longer bear the coalyard work. I thought that whatever happened to me might or might not be an improvement in my working conditions. I did not know what to expect. Once we were assembled, the O.D. man—the Jewish policeman in charge—told us that we were going to Oskar Schindler's Emalia factory. Everyone else was excited about this, but at that time I did not know what it meant. I did not know who this Oskar Schindler was or where I was going. I was about eighteen years old at this time.

I mentioned earlier that the Nazis took over the Jewish-owned businesses when they moved into the cities of Poland. They would install a *Volksdeutscher,* a Pole with German roots, as *Treuhänder,* or custodian. That person would siphon off the assets of the business as he was learning how to operate it. Once he understood the business, the Nazis would liquidate the owner and give the business over to the *Treuhänder.*

I learned later that Herr Schindler had been installed as the custodian of a large pots and pans company at Plaszuw by the name of Emalia. Emalia had been owned by a Jewish man named Banker. Herr Schindler wanted to enlarge the company, so he requested additional people to work in the factory. I was among those fortunate enough to be chosen. Herr Schindler was no ordinary *Treuhänder,* though. To our minds, he was something of a living saint. He was a wealthy businessman but he was absolutely disgusted with the Nazi regime and with what they were doing to the Jews. He took very special care of the Jews who were brought to work for him. Thanks to him, thousands of Jews, myself among them, survived the rest of the ordeal of the camps. He gave us food, he gave us protection, and he gave us hope. I cannot say enough about what a great man he was.

As I said, I did not know anything about Herr Schindler before I got there. I somehow had the feeling that it would be much better for me when they lined us up to go there. My friends told me that it was going to be good. By the time I arrived at Emalia, I knew of his reputation. When I arrived, though, I couldn't believe what I saw. You could roam around the camp. This was unheard of anywhere else. You could walk around, and nobody bothered you. There were no Nazi or Ukrainian soldiers roaming around the camp. I was surprised to see that the atmosphere was so unrestricted.

I saw Herr Schindler almost every day when he was on the camp premises. I saw him while I was at work. He would check with the kitchen. I guess he checked to make sure there was enough food for all the people there. He greeted me when he saw me. He nodded his head. I greeted him in return. This was unimaginable in any other concentration camp. I was not so close that I would go over to him, but nobody, myself included, ran away when they saw him. Nobody was afraid of him. It

Herr Oskar Schindler, righteous Gentile among the nations
(b: 1908; d: 1974)

Oskar Schindler and Abe Zuckerman,
New York City, 1957

seemed that he respected every one of us. He gave us a protective, fatherly feeling. He was always immaculately dressed. He was a very handsome person, like a statesman. I remember that in wintertime, he wore a fur coat. The fur was on the outside, which was a very rare sight for me. In Europe at that time, only men from noble ranks wore coats with fur on the outside. It symbolized great wealth and grandeur, both of which he possessed. He had horses and expensive cars. When I saw him, I felt good. I saw a man who was really taking care of us. With him, I felt, I might survive.

Many years later, after the war ended, I heard him describe his feelings about the war this way: "I hated the brutality, the sadism and the insanity of Nazism. I just couldn't stand by and see people destroyed. I did what I could, what I had to do, what my conscience told me I must do. That's all there is to it. Really. Nothing more." As you can imagine, this was an extraordinary way for a person to feel. He had known Jewish people when he was growing up and he felt compassion for us when the war began and the Nazis began their brutality and killing. Herr Schindler built decent barracks for his Jewish workers. He even smuggled his workers' wives, parents, and children into the camp he ran. He would hide them until the Jewish underground made it possible for them to escape Nazi-occupied territory. On the High Holidays, he saw to it that challah bread was distributed. When a Jewish worker died of illness at the camp, Herr Schindler even arranged for a Jewish burial service.

I later learned that in 1945, when the war was about to end, Herr Schindler gave a party for his workers in the camp and told them that "it was all over." He even gave guns and rifles to a small group of prisoners so they could protect the others in case the retreating Nazi army came through the camp to kill everyone. In my life, I have never come face-to-face with a more courageous, decent, and brilliant man. It goes without saying that I owe my life to him, but I am getting ahead of my story.

At Emalia, Herr Schindler's factory, as far as I knew, there were three divisions. In one part of the factory, the workers manufactured porcelain pots and pans. In the second part of the factory, they were making shells for bullets. The third division was construction. The Simmons company had contracted to do the job of extending Herr Schindler's factory. I was assigned to work on the addition to the factory. I just took whatever job they assigned me. It was hard work, but I felt different about it because nobody stood with the whip above me to make sure I did the work.

Abe and Oskar Schindler at the Western Wall in Jerusalem, 1969

To be honest, I don't know why I was assigned to Herr Schindler's Emalia factory. I guess he needed some more workers. It might have been because of my skills as an electrician. When I was assigned to him, though, my life changed. It was as though I was no longer under the same sort of Nazi administration. I was treated differently. They gave me enough food. I had decent sleeping quarters. In Poland, winters were very harsh. Even in Herr Schindler's camp, I did not get enough warm clothes. I still had my uniform from Julag camp, and it was not a very warm uniform. In order to keep warm, I had to wrap empty cement bags in three or four layers around my body, underneath my jacket. This would not have been permissible at any other camp. The camp barracks were located on the same premises as the factory, so I did not have to travel to work. No trucks, no railroad cars, which had been an everyday torture at the other camps. It was completely different from the other camps. Even the schedule for the work was completely different, because Herr Schindler had ordered it that way.

Here is a typical day at the construction site. We got up early. We got our food. As soon as we finished eating, we went to work. We worked at least ten hours. We did a lot. I tried to conserve my strength. I kept my eyes on the watchmen. When they were not looking, we did not have to work as hard. The work didn't go away; it was always there. The project did not seem to have a time schedule—we did not have to finish by a particular time. As a matter of fact, when I left Herr Schindler, the factory addition still wasn't finished. Herr Schindler did not insist that the addition had to be done by any certain time; he just bided the time together with us. He wanted to stretch out the work for as long as possible, to keep his workers—his people—with him. This was a sign to the Nazis that he needed us. It was his way of keeping us from deportation to the death camps.

While I was working in Herr Schindler's camp, it was possible for me to talk to the other workers. There were ways to talk. I couldn't complain about conditions because that did me no good. I had to accept what I got, but compared to the other camps, it wasn't too bad. I did not have to work as hard for Herr Schindler as I did in Julag or the other camps. Most important, I was never hungry. When you're not hungry, somehow life is bearable. Sometimes I worked until ten at night. For instance, when railroad cars arrived with cement, we had to unload it. The next day we didn't get up as early to work again, because we had worked so many hours the night before. This would never have happened in any other camp I had been in. This is the way Herr Schindler treated his people. I was very surprised to find decent, humane treatment in a concentration camp.

At Herr Schindler's factory, there were mountains of potatoes. This was due to Herr Schindler's thinking of his people. I was told that he used to take truckloads of pots and pans and he would trade them with the Polish farmers for potatoes and other kinds of food. This way, he would have enough food for his people. You have to remember that he risked his life in order to protect the lives of the people working for him. This is why I call him a living saint.

I could always take some potatoes from the factory yard, bring them inside the factory, peel them, and put them in water. I could cook them because the kilns for the glazing of the ceramics had rims on the outside, and those rims were always red-hot. If I put the pot with the potatoes there, in ten minutes I had cooked potatoes. That really kept me alive and not hungry. Nobody ever accused me of stealing when I took the potatoes. It must have been Herr Schindler's orders.

I don't know whether it made sense for an employer to treat workers in a forced labor camp so well. Again, it was Oskar Schindler who did it and nobody else but Oskar Schindler. To me, as I said before, he was a living saint. Because of him I was treated like a human being. And because of him, I was physically able to survive my other ordeals when I was shipped to Mauthausen, the next stop for me after Emalia/Plaszuw. I was a person when I came to Mauthausen, I wasn't what they called a *Muselmann*, an extremely thin person. A *Muselmann* was what they called people who were skinny, dehydrated, dried out—ready for the crematorium.

Oskar Schindler managed somehow to outsmart the Nazi

Above:
Oskar Schindler on one of the many streets named in his honor

Left:
Abe standing in front of a street that he named in honor of Oskar Schindler

administration, to keep them happy, and to keep them from investigating conditions inside the camp. We did not know how he kept the Nazis from finding out that he was taking such good care of us. For example, the Nazi higher-ups often conducted inspections of the camp. Herr Schindler always gave us advance notice of these inspections. When the day arrived, I could see the high Nazi officers at the gate. But Herr Schindler managed somehow to keep the Nazi officers from entering the camp. He would take them to his quarters, where, I heard, he would wine them and dine them. Somehow, they would not enter the camp itself to see what was going on. When they would leave, then we could relax again. This is how much effort he put into protecting his people.

I don't think that Herr Schindler could have done more than he did. He took care of his workers. Everybody was fed well. There was a real infirmary. If anyone was sick, Herr Schindler saw to it that he was given good medical care, as much as was possible. In the other camps where I had been interned, this did not exist. If you went to the infirmary, you were a dead person. If you were not well enough to work, the Nazis would kill you. My friend Yekel Fuhrer became very sick at Plaszuw. If it weren't for his being in Herr Schindler's Emalia camp, I don't know whether he would have survived.

The Avenue of the Righteous in Yad Vashem, Israel, where Oskar Schindler is honored

Oskar Schindler's tombstone at the Mount of Olives Cemetery, Jerusalem. The inscription in Hebrew reads, "Righteous among the nations." The inscription in German below it reads, "The unforgettable savior of 1200 Jews."

1944: Mauthausen

ONE DAY IN AUGUST, 1944, ALL THE GOOD things that I had in Herr Schindler's camp came to an end for me. I was about nineteen years old then. Half of Herr Schindler's Emalia workers were taken away from him. Unfortunately, I was one of those taken away. As for the events leading up to that day, nothing unusual went on. Then the trucks came. We were assembled at the assembly place in the yard outside the barracks. They took half of the prisoners, including me, by truck to the railroad station. It was a surprise to me that I was leaving Herr Schindler—I had no advance warning.

They took us to the railroad station and they loaded us up into railroad cars—cattle cars, really. The cars were so crowded that everyone had to stand. There was no place to sit. Of course, they locked the doors behind us. When the railroad cars were filled, the Nazis moved them to a side track. We must have been there for two or three days. It was the middle of the summer and the heat was unbearable. We were not fed. We were given no water to drink. After a couple of days, I looked through the little windows in the railroad car and I was able to see Herr Schindler coming to the railroad station. As soon as he arrived, he ordered some people—I don't know who they were—to hook up hoses to the water hydrants. He then ordered them to spray the cars with cold water to cool down the cars and alleviate the heat. We were still sitting there in the closed cattle cars. People began to suffocate. A lot of them became dehydrated, and a lot of them died of hunger and thirst. I did not expect to survive this ordeal. After a few days, the railroad cars finally started to move.

We started to move at night. We did not know where we were going, but at least we were moving. By morning, the train stopped and they gave us water. They opened up the cars. There were many dead bodies in the cars because we had neither food nor water all that time. We had no air to breathe. A lot of people even drank their own urine. More people died of dehydration and of starvation. This was probably the Nazis' intent—leaving us so long without water, air or food.

While the train was moving at high speed, a few people were able to crawl out through the little windows of the cattle car and jump out. I don't know what happened to them. I think there was a guard on the outside of each second car. The Nazis had constructed a special little booth for the guard on the rear of each second railroad car. The mood in the train was one of resignation. There was no fear and there was no panic. Everybody was just resigned. The cattle cars were very crowded. As the journey continued, more and more people died.

The stench was unbearable. It was impossible to move the corpses. The train stopped again, but they did not remove the dead from the railroad cars. I cannot tell you where we were when the train stopped. I remember that they gave us water again. The water tasted horrible. After that, they locked the cars and we were moving again, we were going and going. I did not know where I was headed. I only found out on arrival that the destination was the concentration camp at Mauthausen. There we were unloaded and the dead were left behind. We were mostly young people—teenagers. There were very few older people among us. We were ordered to sit on the street and wait. We did not get any food or water while the train was in motion.

Main gate, Mauthausen concentration camp, 1987

The only times we received water were on some occasions when the train stopped.

Upon our arrival at Mauthausen camp, we sat on the street for hours and then we were all ordered to remove our clothes. We were ordered to go to the showers, which were in the basement of a building. I was fearful. I didn't know whether it was really a shower or whether it would be gas. By this point, I knew that they would often fool you—they would tell you to go to the showers, but it would really be cyanide gas. Fortunately, this time, it was a real shower. Afterwards, a man sheared my hair with a barber's clipper. Then he shaved a two-inch strip across my forehead from the front to the back of my head. This was done so that if I ran away, I would be recognized. Not that it was easy to run away, of course. He also shaved every hair I had on my body—under the arms, around the testicles, everywhere. He did the same thing to all the other prisoners.

A view of Mauthausen concentration camp, 1987

After this was done, we were forced to walk naked to another barrack. Then a couple of bullies put me up on a table and examined me internally to see if I might have smuggled any diamonds, or money, or other valuables. This was done to all the other prisoners as well. After all this was done, they gave each of us clothing. They gave me a heavy red jacket that probably had been captured from the Russians. Can you imagine having to wear winter clothes—winter uniforms—in Austria, in the middle of the summer? We had to do all the work the Nazis required of us while wearing those heavy red uniforms.

Most of the prisoners were Jews, but there were also prisoners who were Russians, Poles, Frenchmen, Italians, Greeks—people of all nationalities, Jews and non-Jews. In the morning after my arrival, and after all the indignities and insults I had to go through, I was assigned to work in a big quarry called

"Wienergraben." Mauthausen was located in a high area up in the mountains and the drive to it was very, very beautiful—I visited it forty-three years later, and was struck by the great beauty of the area. But the work in this quarry was inhumane and very hard.

The quarry was on the camp premises. The work consisted of bringing stones up from the quarry. I had to go down one hundred and eighty-six steps into the quarry, pick up a big stone, put it on my shoulder, and go up again. I had to do this constantly—day in, day out, every day, together with all the other prisoners. I was made to work as many hours as the day allowed. The stones were pretty big. You couldn't pick up a small stone. The *kapo*, one of the guards the Nazis used, was there with his stick and you could get a good beating if you were caught with a smaller stone. I was always afraid of getting beaten up. So I had to suffer.

I don't know whether I was brought to Mauthausen to work or to be killed. The work that I did was not especially worthwhile. I think they brought me there to torture me, to demoralize me, to get me weak. So I guess I was probably brought there to be killed. I always say that I survived not because I outsmarted the Nazis, or anything like that, but only because the war ended. In the camps where I was confined, I don't think there were any heroes. The only reason that I survived is because the war ended and I was liberated as the Nazis retreated. Sure, I tried to avoid many dangerous situations in order to survive. But if the war had lasted another six months, *nobody* would have survived, myself included. It would have been impossible to survive even six more months in the conditions I had to endure at Mauthausen.

Fortunately, I was not in Mauthausen that long. From there I was transported, by truck to Gusen II, one of the forty-nine satellite camps of Mauthausen. Incidentally, I learned recently that Fred Friendly, at the time a CBS News reporter, was the first one to arrive in Mauthausen after the Americans liberated it. He

Abe and Millie Zuckerman at the famous death steps leading to the quarry in Mauthausen, 1987

was the first to see the horrors of what the Nazis did. When he spoke about it afterwards he said he could vomit from what he saw there. He also said later that whenever he got back to Austria he came to Linz, and he always goes to visit Mauthausen. If, during the war, you could have spoken to the people who lived near the camp, they would have denied that anything like slave labor was going on in Mauthausen. There was no such place as Mauthausen, they would have told you. But how could they have avoided the stench of the crematorium?

10. August 1944 vom KL. Plaszow

– 94 –

E 13/1

87287	Poln.Jude	Zonenszajn	Szmul	15.8.15	B.Schlosser	Linz III 27/8
288		Zuckermann	Josef	29.7.04	Riemer	Quarz 5/12
289		Zuckerman	Natan	29.12.02	Schäftenm.	"
290		Zuckerberg	Josef	21.1.07	Beamter	Gus.Bergkr.23.3.4[illegible]
291		Zucker	Jakob	1.6.00	A.Mechan.	5.2.45 gest.
292		Zucker	Bernard	26.7.15	Elektr.	Linz III 27/8
293		Zuckerman	Abraham	1.12.24	Aero-Elektr.	Gusen,Messer 13.3.
294		Zweig	Herman	22.7.11	M.Schlosser	Linz III 27/8
295		Zwetschkenstiel	Dawid	13.4.09	H.Arb.	22.11.44 [illegible]
296		Zwick	Joachim	14.1.16	Maler	Gusen,Bergkr.27/8
297		Zylberberg	Chaim	1.11.16	Schneider	"
298		Zylberberg	Izak	23.8.06	Schuster	"
299		Zylberman	Abram	15.6.98	Schneider	19.2.45 gest.
300		Zylbersztajn	Abram	1.2.09	Schuster	7.3.45 gest.
301		Ablöser	Juda	8.10.20	Schneider	Quarz 26.3.44
302		Ablöser	Leser	30.6.19	Schneider	16.1.45 gest.
303		Abraham	Benjamin	2.4.92	Schneider Farber	22.12.44 gest.
304		Abrahamer	Maks	26.1.25	Buerstenb.	13.4.45 gest.
305		Abramowicz	Jakob	[illegible]	[illegible]	[illegible]
306		[illegible]	[illegible]	[illegible]	[illegible]	
307					[illegible]	[illegible] gest.
308					[illegible]	
309		[illegible]	[illegible]	[illegible]	[illegible]	[illegible] gest.
310		[illegible]	[illegible]	[illegible]	[illegible]	[illegible]
311		[illegible]	[illegible]	[illegible]	[illegible]	

Öffentliches Denkmal und Museum Mauthausen
Archiv

List of new arrivals, August 10, 1944, from Plaszuw.
Abe is "Poln. Jew," or Polish Jew, no. 87293.

Courtesy Mauthausen Museum Archives

1944: Gusen II

IF THE CONCENTRATION CAMP AT Mauthausen was horrible, Gusen II extermination camp was even worse. Gusen II was located about four kilometers from Mauthausen. At Gusen II, the killing went on constantly, day and night, killing and burning and drowning and choking. I guess that's why they took the prisoners from Mauthausen there, myself included. Every day at Gusen II, when I got up in the morning and was taken out to work on an open train car, the crematorium was going full-blast. The stench was unbearable. And when I came back from work at night, there was another mountain of dead bodies waiting to be put in the crematorium. This went on every day of the week, during my entire time there. How many people were killed every day, I cannot tell you. But there must have been hundreds of additional bodies piled up every day near the crematorium. We couldn't miss the sight, because the railroad line that took us to work ran alongside the crematorium.

I recently went back to Gusen II, but there was nothing left of the camp. It had been leveled by the Austrians. I was told that 67,000 people perished there and only 2,000 walked out alive, mostly sick and undernourished, myself included.

At Gusen II, I met some of the same people I had known in Plaszuw. I also met some people I knew from home in Cracow.

Some of them are here today in the United States. At Gusen II, I met my friend Alex Beer, whom I had known when I was a little boy in Cracow. One of the men I met at Gusen II, Barry Tiger, works with me today. At Gusen II, as at Mauthausen, I was with prisoners from all countries—Jews, Russians, Frenchmen, Greeks, Yugoslavians, and Italians, people from all over the world. The weakest people in the camp physically were the Jews, the Italians, and the Frenchmen. Somehow, the people from the Slavic countries—the Russians, the Poles, and the Yugoslavs—were the strongest. I guess they were accustomed to a rougher life. In fact, sometimes, when a Russian got a piece of bread, he would exchange it for a cigarette whenever we got a ration of cigarettes. Sometimes, not very frequently, we could get a few cigarettes. The less hardy prisoners would never have done that. They would have kept the bread and eaten it.

You might wonder how we were able to communicate if we all spoke different languages. During my confinement, I learned almost all the languages of Europe. I learned the necessary words and phrases so that I could communicate with the other people. Some of the prisoners only spoke Yiddish, so I spoke Yiddish with them. I spoke German to the Nazis when it was necessary, Russian with the Russians, and so on. Somehow I learned all the languages in the camp. We had to communicate, so we learned each other's languages.

Sometimes, at Gusen II, the prisoners were able to talk to each other. We conversed whenever possible. We talked while marching to work, in the barracks, or on the job. There was always something to talk about. For example, we would talk about how many people had gotten twenty-five or fifty lashes when they stood in line for a second serving of coffee that morning. The kapos were sadistic and acted violently. They got some of their sadistic fun at the morning meal. They would announce, "Whoever wants another cup of black coffee, line up." So everyone would run to be the first on line. That's when

Barracks at Gusen II

the beatings began. I got caught in this melee once. A kapo hit me in the head when I went forward for a second cup of coffee. It was a severe blow. My head was swollen for quite a few weeks. I suffered for quite some time until the pain subsided.

The line would get unruly and the kapos would start swinging their rubber sticks at people's heads. Sometimes the kapos did all this intentionally, in order to satisfy their sadistic desires. I would hide in between the *pritches* (bunks) and just watch and try to avoid trouble. The time they hit me in the head, I suffered for weeks until the pain stopped. That was the last time I went back for seconds. From then on, I only watched from the side. They would also take people out of the line for no reason whatsoever and give them lashes. So as you can see, we had plenty to talk about each day.

When I arrived at Gusen II, we were all lined up and the Nazis asked for the occupations of each of the prisoners. I told them that I was an electrician, as I always did whenever I was moved to a different camp. Fortunately for me, they assigned me to special jobs. At Gusen II, I was assigned to work in the nearby town of St. Georgian. There were mountains in St. Georgian and the Nazis were using the prisoners as forced labor to build tunnels through these mountains. They called these tunnels *Shtollen.*

We called the tunnels, or *Shtollen,* under construction "St. Georgian." The tunnels took their name from the nearby town of St. Georgian, Austria. The tunnels were built for the sole purpose of housing aircraft assembly lines. At the worksite, one group was assigned to dig and construct the tunnels, cementing them and bracing them. Another group worked on an aircraft assembly line located inside the tunnels. These tunnels looked like the Holland or Lincoln Tunnels, going through the mountains. I guess the purpose of having the factories in the tunnels was to hide the aircraft production from bombardment.

In the *Shtollen* I was assigned to work on the aircraft assembly line, where they were manufacturing V-2 rockets and fighter planes for the Messerschmidt company. My part of the work was to assemble the cockpits of fighter planes. I told them I was a craftsman, so they assigned me to the planes. At least that way I did not have to work at hard labor. I was fortunate to work on the fighter planes and not on the construction of the tunnels, which was much harder work and was much more dangerous. Many times the bracing of the tunnel under construction would collapse. The tunnel would cave in and many people would be buried alive.

As I said, I worked on an assembly line for the Messerschmidt company. The line moved along, and every time I finished my job it was moved further to the next person. The work was supervised by private foremen from the Messerschmidt company, not by the Nazis. Often, though, the Nazis would come in to see how the work was coming along. Sometimes they would beat the prisoners, myself included.

Often, we could not work because there were no parts—they

Abe at Gusen II, 1987. The famous *Shtollen* (tunnels) at St. Georgian that housed the Messerschmidt aircraft factory where Abe worked during his incarceration at Gusen II are now being dismantled by the Austrian government to erase the memories.

A translation of the inscription on the monument, *opposite,* reads:

At the time of the Nazi suppression thousands of inmates from the KZ's Mauthausen and Gusen II were forced to work at hard slave labor in these underground shafts. Those structures were commonly known as cellar dwellings.
Tired and destroyed through this terrible exhausting struggle and the daily brutality they had soon only one real freedom left: the freedom to die.
The great illuminating memory of their holy sacrifices gives us absolutely no reason for division and hate, but it is a reason for a new order, for peace and the unity of all peoples to again work together.

Monument at the entrance to the *Shtollen* at St. Georgian. A translation of the inscription appears *opposite.*

might have been missing tools or rivets. At other times there were air raids—a bombing alarm, so the electricity had to be cut off. The air raids increased in frequency in early 1945, as the war was coming to an end. The lights would be off in the tunnels for two or three hours, or sometimes for a whole day, so I just sat there, in the dark, in the cockpit of a fighter plane.

I worked without food. I was fed in the morning and then again when I got back from work. I got coffee in the morning and I don't remember what else. I don't know how little I weighed, but I was losing weight and I was losing my strength. When we got back to the camp at the end of every work day, they gave us soup made from potato peels and some kind of fat mixed in. The soup was barely edible. But I was hungry, so what could I do?

When I first arrived at Gusen II, during the early months, we were given one loaf of bread for every two prisoners as we marched in from work. However, as the war continued, there was less and less food for the prisoners. The culmination was one loaf of bread for twenty-four people. The bread was so crushed that they had to give it to us in a bowl. Twenty-four people would be grabbing to get a few crumbs from this bowl. Again, I stayed away from the people grabbing the crumbs because I was afraid to get a beating. I took my soup and I went to my *pritch,* and I ate it there. I knew that nothing good could come out of the commotion surrounding the loaf of bread. Only beatings and more beatings.

Hunger and starvation were so bad at Gusen II that some of the prisoners who worked in the *Shtollen* actually ate a black substance of some kind that they found in one of the layers of dirt that they exposed while digging. I remember seeing these men as we lined up to go back to the barracks at the end of the day. Their mouths were black from the dirt they ate.

Messerschmidt company foremen, who were civilian engineers, saw the atrocities that were committed against us.

Sometimes, some of them tried to help us. The foreman in charge of my part of the work was compassionate. He was a nice guy. Sometimes he would bring me a piece of bread. This helped a lot. The foremen were afraid to help us—they probably would have been criticized if they had been caught. The Nazis walked around the *Shtollen.* The foreman who brought me bread would take me far away from the other people, so that no one would see what he was doing. I remember he was a short, skinny person. He had a good heart. He was very careful not to be caught.

We traveled from the camp to the workplace in open railroad cars. Sometimes, when the rain came down, we went to the railroad car in knee-deep mud. We had to make it to the cars any way we could. The Nazis, with their riding whips, and the kapos, with their rubber sticks, would chase us. When I was first assigned to work on the aircraft in the *Shtollen,* I had no shoes at all. Then the Nazis brought in shoes from somewhere—they gave everyone wooden shoes. We called them *Hollanderkis*—shoes from Holland that Dutch people wear. These were extremely painful for me to walk in. That was the most horrible situation for me, to walk and to work in these wooden shoes. Then one day, one of the soldiers came in and he brought us regular leather shoes. I was lucky to get a pair. I was so relieved to know that I wouldn't have to wear those painful wooden shoes any longer. It was a great relief for me.

My new leather shoes were so important to me that I had to watch them constantly because other prisoners might steal them while I was sleeping. So at night I would take my shoes and wrap around them the clothing I had, and I would sleep on top of the bundle to make sure that I still had shoes in the morning. If you had no shoes at all, and a lot of people had no shoes, you were a sorry person. You would have to walk barefoot in all the mud, the stones, the rocks, and everything else. It was impossible.

There was little else for the prisoners to steal. Either a piece of bread that someone was hiding, or cigarettes, or your shoes.

Whoever smoked looked for cigarettes. When the smokers could not obtain cigarettes, they would take leaves from trees. They would put the leaves under their straw mattresses and keep them there until they dried. When the leaves dried, they would crush them and roll them up in pieces of paper—mostly bits of newspaper lying around in the streets on the way to work. If they could not find newspaper, they would use whatever paper they could find. Then they would smoke the "cigarettes" they had made. Aside from these few things, there was nothing to steal among the prisoners. You had to watch your clothing, and your shoes, and sometimes a piece of bread, if you had one that you had not eaten yet.

Except for stealing from one another occasionally, the prisoners at Gusen II generally treated each other as well as they could under the stressful circumstances. As far as I know, there were no informers among the prisoners at Gusen II. I don't think there was anything to inform about. No one informed on anyone. Everybody was *of gehakte tsuris*—the Yiddish expression meaning that we were all in the same predicament. In Plaszuw I knew I could never trust the other prisoners, but at Gusen II there were no informers. By this time I had learned not to talk, to tell stories, because that could only bring you problems. At Gusen II, the prisoners spoke to each other without fear. This was very different from what went on in Plaszuw. At Plaszuw, some of the prisoners thought they could save themselves from deportation or somehow get better treatment by collaborating with the Nazis. By the time I had been brought to Gusen II, though, I had seen that the collaborators were killed along with everyone else—with no exceptions. Collaborating did not save anyone.

In Gusen II, everyone was equal. There were only kapos and *Stubenältester,* the kapos' supervisors. The kapos, as I mentioned earlier, were guards the Nazis used to keep watch on the prisoners. The kapos themselves were convicts—people who had been convicted of crimes like murder. Above the kapos were the

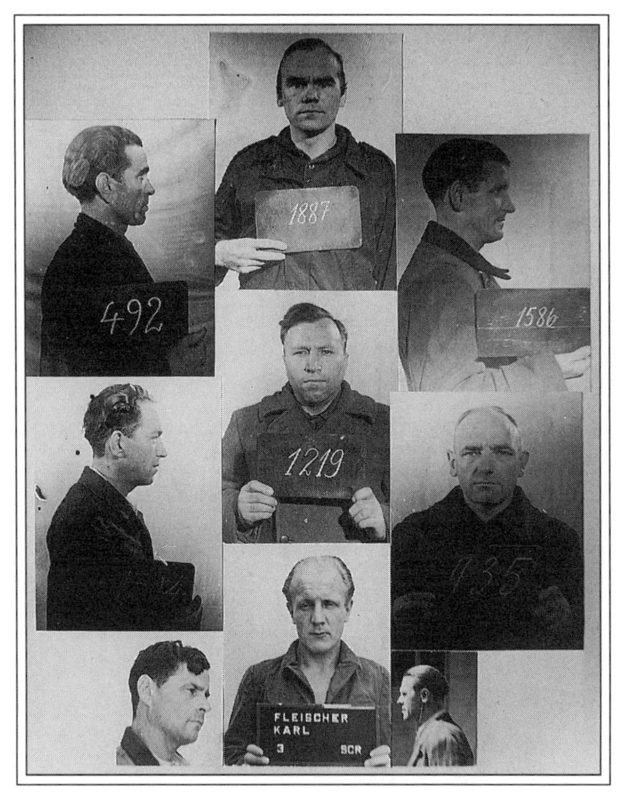

Gusen II kapos on trial, Dachau, 1946

Stubenältester, who lived in the barracks with us and who were in charge of keeping order in the barracks.

Also in the barracks, in addition to the Jewish prisoners, were prisoners of all different nationalities, including some Poles. One time, on a Sunday, when we didn't go to work, I heard a lot of yelling at the front of the barrack. The barrack had a hall two or three hundred feet long with *pritches* (bunks) on either side. It contained at least three hundred people. It seems that there were some Polish prisoners who really thought of themselves as the elite among the prisoners. However, they detested the Jews. Imagine, they had to live together with Jews! When I heard this crying and yelling, I lay on my bed hiding. I did not know what was going on. I found out later that the Poles had been hanged, or had to hang themselves, from rafters in our barrack. I think the kapos gave them ropes and the Poles had to hang themselves, for what reason I don't know. There were seven or eight of them. They must have done something to anger the Nazis. The Nazis must have given the orders to the kapos.

To give you another example of the kind of horrors that went on at Gusen II, there was the day of *Entlausung,* the delicing. Although I went through the *Entlausung* a couple of times when they gassed the buildings to get rid of the lice, this one was especially horrible. It happened in January, 1945. On the night before we were deloused, the Nazis ordered us all to undress. The kapos examined each and every one of us. Whoever had blemishes on his body, no matter what kind, was taken outside by the kapos. One kapo would hit the person over the head with a blunt object. Then the two kapos would pick him up and put him head first in a barrel of water, until he drowned. This went on for a whole night. Hundreds and hundreds of prisoners were killed that night in every barrack throughout the camp. I tried to hide wherever I could. I went to the other end of the barrack. Somehow I tried to avoid the grabbing. In the morning, I saw piles and piles of dead bodies.

Then, that next morning, the survivors were ordered out of the barracks. They moved us to another barrack. They were using gas in the barracks to get rid of the lice and bedbugs. That took a whole day and a whole night. We just sat on the floor, one in front of the other, legs spread. Then, the next day, they chased us from the barracks to a building that contained the showers. It was at least a ten-minute run to that other building. Remember, this was in the dead of winter. They had us running naked, through ice and snow, to the showers. I cannot tell you the temperature, but we were running on ice. That will give you an idea of how cold it was.

When I finally got to the showers, there were two bullies

with water hoses. They hosed me down and then I had to run back to the barrack, where I was shaved again, all over my body. And they again shaved off a strip of hair down the center of my head. Then they gave me new clothing—a new striped uniform with a hat. Later on, they sent us back to work, to the *Shtollen.*

While all this was going on, I never really thought about the future. I didn't think my life would ever change. I thought this was the way life would always be for me, if I survived. Whenever I was coming to work or coming back to the barracks, and I saw the mountains of dead people, I would think to myself, next I'm going to be dead, and I'm going to lie there on the piles. I never thought that my life as a prisoner would end and that life would be normal again. I don't know why I felt this way. Maybe it's because I went into the camps at a young age and I thought that this was the way life was.

While I was in the camps, I did not know much about the political leaders of the time. I did not know who Churchill was, but I did know who President Roosevelt was—I knew he was the "President of America," as we called him then. One day, while I was at work, I heard one of the foremen from the Messerschmidt company say in German that "our father" had died. He meant that President Roosevelt had died. It really didn't mean anything to me, because I didn't see any difference in the camps while Roosevelt was alive. I don't think he helped much while I was in the worst of the camps.

During the spring of 1945, representatives of the Red Cross sent food packages into the camp. This was the first time we had ever received these sorts of packages. Each one of us got a package containing canned goods, food, and cigarettes. I remember there were cigarettes because I traded the cigarettes with another prisoner for a piece of bread. I was very surprised to get a package. I didn't expect anything like it. I was starving, and here, to my surprise, was a package of food. When I saw the package, I didn't believe what I was seeing. I couldn't believe that someone knew about us and our plight well enough to send us food. I thought that no one in the world knew about us.

Shortly after I received the Red Cross package, the Nazis in the camp began to spread a rumor that we would be freed and that we would go to Switzerland. The Nazis selected a few hundred people to go. Somehow, I was not one of them. I might not have been chosen because they often chose people alphabetically and my last name starts with a "Z." I regretted that they did not select me. It turned out, however, that not being chosen actually worked to my benefit. I found out after I was liberated from the camp that these people had really been selected for a death march. The ones selected were forced to walk to a town called Gunskirchen. I am not sure, but I was told that they went from there to Auschwitz. The whole thing was a Nazi ploy. They never saw Switzerland.

Once again, I was able to survive an ordeal by sheer luck, by not being counted in. Shortly after this event, Gusen II camp was liberated by the American army.

About three weeks before the liberation, things began to change in the camp. The Nazis, in conjunction with the kapos who lived with us inside the barracks, introduced new rules every day. One day, they told us that we were not going out to work that day. Instead, we stayed inside. Then, the next day, they gave us very little food. Then they announced that in order to go the latrine, we had to be escorted in groups of ten. I did not know the reason for these changes, but somehow I sensed that something was going to happen. I did not know *when,* though, and I did not know what was going to happen. I don't know whether we were going to be moved again, or liberated, or killed. I was especially fearful because, during the last few weeks of work in the *Shtollen,* they were digging holes at the entrances to the tunnels. I thought the holes were going to be filled with explosives so that they could bring us all in, set off the explosives, and kill us all.

Abe (far right) at the War Crimes Trials in Dachau, Germany, 1947, with his friend Alex Beer (left) and another witness

I stayed in the barracks. When I looked outside, I saw a lot of activity. I saw planes roaming the skies and tanks running in the fields. I also saw that the Nazi guards had left and that they had given authority over the concentration camp to the local police. The Austrian police took over the job of manning the guard towers. I don't know how I survived this period, because, as I said, there was even less food than before, when we had been going to work. I know we were all very hungry and tired. During the last week before liberation, there was no administration at all. The administration had fled. Even the Austrian police, who were supposed to guard us, had all run off. During those last few days, I just didn't eat at all. No one ate.

Abraham Zuckerman (L) with War Crimes Chief Prosecutor, Jules L. Druss, 1st Lt., his aide and three survivor/witnesses.

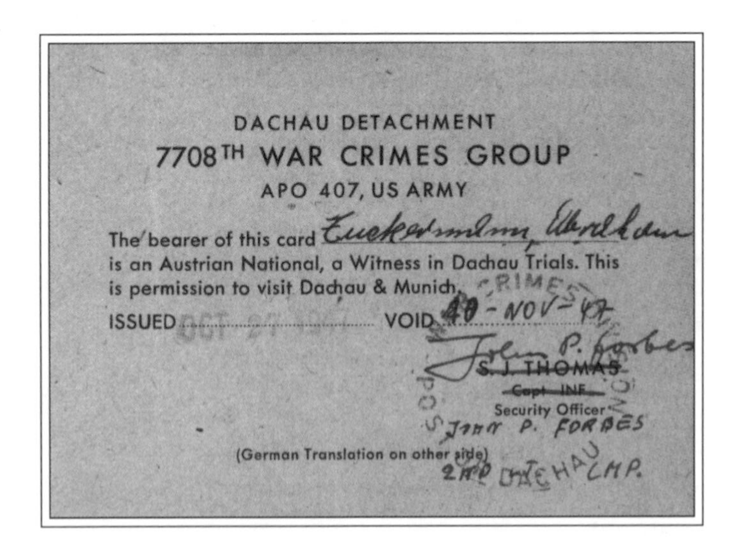

DACHAU DETACHMENT
7708TH WAR CRIMES GROUP
APO 407, US ARMY

The bearer of this card Zuckermann, Abraham
is an Austrian National, a Witness in Dachau Trials. This
is permission to visit Dachau & Munich.

ISSUED OCT 24 1947 VOID 30 - NOV - 47

John P. Forbes
~~S. J. THOMAS~~
~~Capt INF~~
Security Officer
John P. Forbes
2nd Dachau CMP.

(German Translation on other side)

Abe's identification document as a witness at the War Crimes Trials in Dachau, Germany

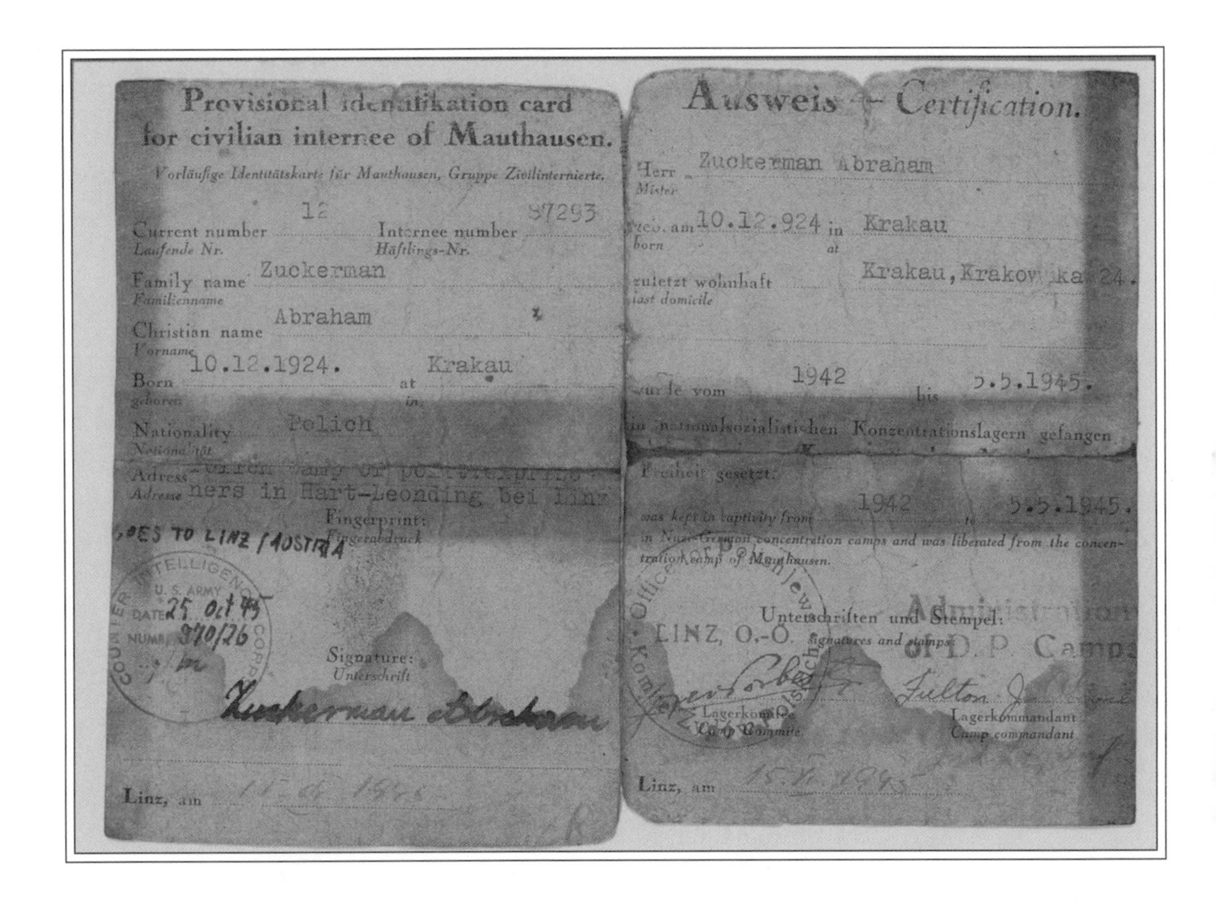
Provisional identifikation card
for civilian internee of Mauthausen.
Vorläufige Identitätskarte für Mauthausen, Gruppe Zivilinternierte.

Current number / Laufende Nr.: 12
Internee number / Häftlings-Nr.: 87293
Family name / Familienname: Zuckerman
Christian name / Vorname: Abraham
Born / geboren: 10.12.1924. at / in: Krakau
Nationality / Nationalität: Polich
Adress / Adresse: ... ners in Hart-Leonding bei Linz
Fingerprint: / Fingerabdruck

GOES TO LINZ (AUSTRIA

U. S. ARMY
DATE 25 Oct 45
NUMB. 970/26

Signature: / Unterschrift
Zuckerman Abraham

Linz, am 11-6 1946

Ausweis — Certification.

Herr / Mister: Zuckerman Abraham
geb. am / born: 10.12.924 in / at: Krakau
zuletzt wohnhaft / last domicile: Krakau, Krakowska 24.
wurde vom 1942 bis 5.5.1945.
in nationalsozialistischen Konzentrationslagern gefangen ...
Freiheit gesetzt.
was kept in captivity from 1942 to 5.5.1945.
in Nazi-German concentration camps and was liberated from the concentration camp of Mauthausen.

Unterschriften und Stempel: / Signatures and stamps:
LINZ, O.-Ö.
Administration of D.P. Camps
Lagerkomitee / Camp Commite
Lagerkommandant / Camp commandant
Fulton

Linz, am 15.V. 1945

IDENTIFICATION
FOR CIVILIAN INTERNEE OF MAUTHAUSEN

MAY, 1945: LIBERATION—LIBERATION!

ON SATURDAY AFTERNOON, MAY 5, 1945, Gusen II camp was liberated—I will never forget that date. The date is always before me in my memory. At that time, the only thing I knew was that I was no longer under guard. Only two American soldiers arrived in a jeep to liberate a camp containing approximately two thousand prisoners. Just two soldiers, and a jeep with a rotating machine gun, liberated the whole camp. When they arrived, all the prisoners ran to the barbed wire surrounding the camp and dismantled the barbed wire instantly. It was a joyous moment, it is indescribable, really, the moment we were liberated. It was a happy noise—a big roar.

People started running out of the barracks and nobody was there to tell them to come back. Can you imagine? It was a nice, warm spring day. But the sorry thing about the liberation was that I didn't know where to go. I was liberated but I was too weak to walk out of the camp. I was very weak. Believe it or not, that night I slept in the camp.

In fact, liberation was the second saddest day of my life. The saddest day was when I became a "all-around orphan," as the

Yiddish phrase puts it, when they took away my parents and my sisters. The second-saddest day was liberation, and let me explain why. I was a young person. I spent my teen years—six years—under guard and torture. I was twenty and I had been liberated—but to do what? To go where? Where do you go after liberation? My torture started when I was a kid of fourteen, and I walked out six years later at the age of twenty. In many ways I was still the same kid I was at fourteen because I did not know anything else. I really did not know what was on the outside. Imagine. When a soldier goes home from war or active duty, his family waits by the port to greet him. Nobody greeted me. Nobody was waiting for me—no mother, no father, no sisters, no uncles, no aunts. I was all alone. I had no place to go, really. I did not know where I was going. Each of the liberated prisoners was all alone, every one of us. Each of us was one person left from a whole family that had been murdered. It was sad. It was very sad.

When we were liberated, the first thing that happened was that the prisoners carried out a plan that they had conceived in the days before the American soldiers came. All of the prisoners wanted to take revenge on the kapos, who had tortured us and beat us during our confinement in the barracks. I could sense that this would happen. During the last few days before liberation, some of the prisoners were watching the kapos. We learned what they had in mind—they would not let the kapos escape alive from the camp. We all had waited for this day.

The prisoners who were physically the strongest were the first to take vengeance on the kapos. Before the Americans arrived, the kapos went into hiding wherever they could, but the prisoners kept an eye on them. I think the *Stubenführer*, the kapo commandant in our barrack, managed somehow to escape. But the prisoners found the first of the ordinary kapos and they killed him right on the spot. Then they searched the barrack and throughout the camp for the other kapos. Some were hiding up in the rafters and others were hiding under the beds. We pulled them all out, and they were killed, right then and there. The prisoners killed the kapos barehanded, without weapons. They killed them with whatever they had—with their hands, or with wood. There were no weapons in the camp, but they managed to kill them. They made them suffer for all the suffering they had inflicted on us.

Everybody wanted to participate, to take revenge for the beatings and the mutilations, but some of the prisoners were too weak. Some of them could not even walk. The French, the Italian, and the Jewish prisoners were very weak. That was the day everyone had been waiting for, to take revenge on those murderers who had tortured us all this time. We also wanted to keep a promise to our parents that we would take revenge when the time came.

The Nazis—what they did was one thing. They were the authorities in the camp. The kapos went even further than the Nazis in terms of cruelty and torture. The kapos did sadistic things that the Nazis did not even require them to do. For example, a kapo at one point got mad at me because I would not submit to him. His name was Fritz. He was a big bully of a man. He must have weighed over three hundred pounds. Because he was angry at me, he made me squat and hop back and forth in the *Shtollen* where I worked.

This was typical of the unnecessary cruelty of the kapos, who did not have to do all the vicious things they did. I guess they wanted to show the Nazis how "good they were." They died a slow death at the hands of the prisoners. In my own barracks, three kapos were killed.

I also saw the American soldiers collect the remaining Nazi soldiers—the ones who had not managed to leave on time with the rest—as prisoners of war. I saw the Nazis sitting on the ground with their hands behind their heads. The G.I.'s—the American soldiers—collected them and marched them off. This sight did not affect me as much as when they killed the kapos, though. That was my greatest satisfaction, to see revenge taken on those murderers, those bandits who had tortured and killed for so long. You may not be aware that the Nazi soldiers themselves rarely came into the barracks where the Jewish prisoners were kept. The kapos and the *Stubenführer,* the kapo commandant, ran the barracks, and they were in a world by themselves. They ran the barracks as though the barracks were their own territory.

The Americans did not stop any one of us from having whatever revenge we could take. When they entered the camps to liberate us, the Americans saw the masses of dead bodies and sick, starved people. They were so disgusted that they did not stop us. Nobody stopped us. The scene was chaos, really. Everybody was running in a different direction. Some were running out of the camp, some went to the kitchen. You're talking about thousands of people, so it was chaos. As usual, I kept a low profile.

The next thing many of us did was to look for food, because we were very hungry. We had barely eaten for days and I had not eaten anything as substantial as a piece of bread in two weeks. So we went directly to the kitchen, where we found a lot of flour and coffee. I mixed the flour and the coffee. Together, we made a fire, and we made pancakes. The pancakes were not done on a frying pan, they were cooked directly on the fire. Just a couple of pieces of wood. I charred the wood on the outside and then I baked the pancakes, and I ate, just to fill up my stomach. Even this was not enough, but I ate a little bit. I was not afraid at all. I was excited, and I was exhausted. This is how I felt until I could get some more food. Only later did I realize that I had no place to go, really, and I did not know where I was going. I went to my bunk bed and slept until the next morning.

THE DAY AFTER LIBERATION, MAY 6, 1945: LINZ, AUSTRIA

THE NEXT MORNING, THE DAY AFTER liberation, I started to walk with a group of young men my age. We had become friends in camp, and now we had been liberated together. We were guided to walk toward Linz. The American soldiers were already directing us along the roadway. They were stationed about a hundred feet apart. We were walking and walking and walking, and the soldiers were directing us. In between I had to sit down to rest because of weakness. We walked from Gusen II to Linz, which is only about fourteen kilometers, but it took us a whole day. That is how weak and worn out and undernourished I was. I never looked in a mirror to see what I looked like the whole time I was interned, because there had been no mirrors in the camp.

Prisoners by the thousands were walking from all the different camps. There was a concentration camp in every town in Austria. Mauthausen alone, as I mentioned, had forty-nine satellite camps.

As the American army advanced, they liberated each of the concentration camps, so the whole road to Linz was filled with people. We stopped here and there and asked the inhabitants for food. They gave us food. That's how we fed ourselves on the road. But the walk was very hard on me. I was so weak that I had to stop and lie down every hour or so.

I still wore my striped uniform. I still had the shaved stripe on my head. I did not change my clothes on the way to Linz. I felt like a little kid. I really did not comprehend what was going on. I didn't worry, I didn't think about anything. The only thing I wondered was whether I would find anybody from my family alive. I cannot say whether all the prisoners could make the walk. I do not know how many died on the way to Linz because a lot of people died after we were liberated. They died of hunger, dysentery, or some incurable sickness. There were no cars or ambulances to take us out of the camps. Whether the sick people survived, I also cannot say. I did not look back.

The liberation seemed like an unbelievable dream to me. As soon as I was liberated, all the atrocities left me, they just left me. The atrocities were far away and my thinking went in a different direction. I didn't think about what had happened. I only thought, "What now?" The first thing I wanted to do was to see if my family was alive. I also wanted to find a place to eat and a place to sleep. I knew that wherever the American soldiers led us, I would have a place to sleep.

Around five in the afternoon, I reached a tremendous underground bomb shelter at Linz. The American soldiers organized things there. The American army arranged for the local women to bring us old clothing. The Americans gave us food. I took off the striped uniform and I put on a new shirt. Well, I don't know where the shirt came from, but at least it was clean. However it fit, I wore it. It was old clothing and hand-me-downs, but it was better than the striped uniform. The G.I.'s were very friendly and very courteous to us.

While I was in the shelter, I didn't do anything. I rested. The local people who were helping us with clothing and other things had been leading normal lives all this time, while we were in the concentration camps. I guess they tolerated the existence of the concentration camps. They lived within a few kilometers of all this killing and torture, and they must have known what was going on, but they tolerated it. As I said earlier, how could they have avoided the stench of the crematoria? How could they deny what had happened?

Despite all this, I didn't see any incidents between the survivors and the local people. We were all weak and subdued at the time. We were not rabblerousers. We were just quiet. I was only waiting to see what would happen next. I stayed inside there for a few days. I didn't go out because the war was still on and we were afraid that the shelter might be bombed.

I don't think the American soldiers who liberated the concentration camps knew what they would find before they entered. Gusen is a little town, but the camp there was enormous. In fact, there were three camps in Gusen, numbered I, II, and III. They were all satellite camps of Mauthausen. The American soldiers only realized what was happening when they approached the camps because of the stench from the crematorium and the dead bodies lying around. It took the G.I.'s a few days to comprehend the atrocities they saw. They were bitter at what they saw, and I don't blame them. They saw all those piles of dead people, mountains of dead people, and they couldn't do enough to take care of us, the survivors.

They brought us food and more clothing—they would load up the trucks and bring in food and clothing from warehouses. Some of us who spoke English had conversations with them. A lot of the soldiers spoke Yiddish, but we really didn't understand each other. We just used sign language. They really did care for us.

At Linz, they took care of the absolute basics—food, clothing

and shelter. I did not receive medical attention in the shelter in Linz. In the concentration camps, I had been walking around with a toothache for almost two years. I had been afraid to go to the infirmary or to the dentist to have it pulled or treated because nobody would treat it. It was well known in the camps that anyone who went to the infirmary with an illness or injury would be killed immediately by the Nazis. The infirmary was the end of the road, so I was afraid, and I didn't go. I suffered the pain. I was in constant pain for two years.

When I was liberated, and when a little of my strength had returned, the first thing I did was to go to the hospital in Linz. The hospital was run by nuns. I told them in German about my toothache. They had to put me to sleep to pull the tooth. That was the first medical attention I received. After a few days, it healed. My pain stopped. As a result of waiting two years for treatment, the right side of my face remains swollen to this day.

Life in the bunker in Linz was getting a little monotonous. So I joined three friends of mine from the concentration camp and we went out and occupied an apartment in a bombed-out, vacant house. One apartment was still standing and was in good shape. We went around the basements of the bombed-out ruins nearby and we found a lot of stored food—cartons of groceries with all kinds of food products. We brought into the apartment one of my friends, David Werner, who unfortunately is no longer with us. He was the organizer and the cook. We stayed there for two or three weeks. We fed ourselves well because we found a lot of condensed milk. It was thick and sweet like honey. That's what we ate. These living quarters did not last too long. We heard that the people from the bunker were being moved to an estate not far from Linz. We decided to go to the estate, which was called Hart.

We stayed in houses at Hart. It was more *heimlich*—a more homelike environment. People were coming and coming and coming from all over Austria, from the concentration camps liberated by the American soldiers. All I did was ask and inquire of the people I met, did you know this, did you know that, did you see this one, did you see my father, my mother, my sisters, my uncles, anyone. Wherever I went, I wrote on the walls who I was looking for. We all did that—we would write on the walls our names and the names of relatives we hoped to find. That's all I was busy with during the first few weeks. I thought that maybe I would find some relatives alive. But it did not happen that way. No one else survived from my family. I was the only one.

With the help of the American soldiers, we became more and more like human beings again. I don't know how much I weighed. I was a very skinny kid and very undernourished. I was below the normal weight for a twenty-year-old. At the estate in Hart, I was assigned to a room for ten or twelve people. There were just beds. There wasn't much room for anything else. The Americans set up a kitchen and we were fed, and we went to the public baths in Linz to bathe. It was a real pleasure to be free and to be able to take a bath. Can you imagine?

In Hart, after hours, some of us would gather together in one of the rooms and we would sing the old cantorial melodies we remembered from Cracow. I said earlier that there was a very famous *rov*, or rabbi, in Cracow who was called the *Melicer Rav.* He was a great composer of liturgical music. I used to go to his *shul*, his synagogue, to hear him sing on Friday nights. So I knew a lot of his songs, and so did a lot of the other boys at Hart. We would get together and sing the old songs. It meant a lot to me because it gave me a sort of feeling of home.

I started to feel free. I was a young man, and nothing serious was on my mind. I didn't care to hear a single thought about the outside world. I wasn't interested. I still thought that there *was* no outside world. A few days later, I learned that the war in Europe was over—that the Germans had surrendered. This was gratifying news. But I never revisited the concentration camps in my thinking. Even after a few days, it seemed so far away—it was so unbelievable. It was such a horrible experience that I did not want to get it back in my thoughts again. No one in the camp went back in their thoughts.

It was true that I dreamed about home. I dreamed about my home, my parents, my sisters. How could you not dream about your family? But somehow, things do not affect you physically or mentally that much when you're young. When you're young, you think you're immortal, and certain things do not bother you. As you get older, though, you start to feel the pain more and more. The older I get, the more hurt I feel. It all came around full circle for me in the later years. In Hart, I had a few sleepless nights, but most of the time, I didn't have much trouble sleeping. I was so exhausted that I needed to sleep. Somehow the past temporarily left me.

I don't think that any human being in the world can imagine on an emotional level how it felt for me to be free. I still had scars from the camps on my legs and on my hands. These scars had never healed in the concentration camps, because of the bad food and living conditions. Somehow, as soon as I was liberated and I started to consume normal food, my scars healed. In camp, the scars would never heal. They were always very painful.

The emotional scars would not heal as quickly. I missed my family. That was the worst part of my life now, missing my family. I was still thinking and dreaming of my family and my relatives. I couldn't find any of my relatives. You have to understand that six years of my life had been taken away. These are the best years of a young person. These were my teen years. When I was separated from my parents, I really had not gotten to know them very well. In my home in Cracow, I was busy with school all day, from morning to night. I was a kid, so I really had more to do with other kids than with my parents, although my parents were really caring. I wanted more to play with other kids than to be at home, so, in a sense, I really didn't get to know my parents very well.

My parents took very good care of my sisters and me. I mentioned that my mother got up at four in the morning to see that my shoes were clean and shined, that my socks were mended, and that there was coffee and food for all the children. In those days, it wasn't like here in America, where you turn a switch and the oven starts to heat up. There, you had to do it with wood and coals. Sometimes it took my mother hours to get a fire going, to make a cup of coffee or to prepare food.

When all these things were finally done—making the fire, preparing the food, and making coffee, my mother would pack up my lunch for me and I would go off to school. So, as you can see, there was never enough time to be with my parents, to get to know them on a deeper level. I was too young and there was too little time. The Nazis took that time away from me. And now, after the Nazi destruction, I would *never* get to know my parents, who had done so much for my sisters and me.

June 6, 1945: Bindermichel, Austria

AFTER A WHILE, HART BECAME TOO SMALL for the population of newly arriving liberated prisoners. So from Hart we were moved to Bindermichel, a town on the outskirts of Linz. As the Americans were moving through Austria, they liberated more and more camps. So more and more people came to Hart, and Hart could not handle that many people.

We traveled from Hart to Bindermichel in American trucks. It was different, of course, traveling with American soldiers compared to the way we had traveled between the concentration camps. Bindermichel was a settlement of a type of garden apartments. I heard that it had been built by Belgian and Dutch Jewish prisoners during the war for the families of the German soldiers. When the Americans came, they took over the apartments and established a displaced persons (DP) camp in the town of Bindermichel. The American soldiers, with the help of relief organizations like the United Nations Relief and Rehabilitation Administration (UNRRA), the Hebrew Immigrant Aid Society (HIAS), and the Joint Distribution Committee (JDC), brought to Bindermichel survivors from the various death camps and settled them there.

I was in Bindermichel for four years, from June, 1945 to May, 1949. I do not know exactly how many people resided there, but there must have been at least a few thousand refugees. The living conditions were good, especially compared with what I had in the concentration camps. I was young and just happy to be alive. I was without any cares. When I arrived in Bindermichel, I was assigned along with five other young men to a three-bedroom apartment. The apartment consisted of three bedrooms, an all-purpose room, and a bathroom, so we were assigned two boys to a room. At first, in Bindermichel, I didn't do anything all day long. I was recuperating from my ordeal. A lot of the camp survivors needed to be hospitalized, but fortunately, I was in pretty good health, compared with some of the others. I was able to help out some of my friends. I was able to visit some of them, including my friend Yekel Fuhrer, in the hospital.

Soon after I moved into Bindermichel, the Americans set up tents for us. Each tent had a different purpose. There were tents for the kitchen, for entertainment, and for a synagogue. Later on, the tents were replaced with more permanent barracks. Life in Bindermichel was free and easy. Ninety-five percent of the people there were single boys, along with a few single girls. In the whole camp, there were no more than two or three families that had survived the war intact.

In the beginning, I did not believe that there was a world outside the DP camp. I would say that some of us, myself included, lived like kids. We were given food and we were given clothing. We took care of ourselves—for example, I washed my own laundry in the bathtub in my apartment. I didn't have a worry in the world. I didn't want to care about anything. I tried to occupy my mind with thoughts unrelated to the war. For instance, a friend of mine in the DP camp at Bindermichel was a tailor. He was from Dukla, the same town my father came from. I used to go see him and we would sing Yiddish songs together. I would write the lyrics down in a notebook, and I still have those notebooks. I used to visit him quite frequently because I enjoyed our camaraderie. I tried not to think about the horrors I had gone through, because the minute I started to think, all the horrors would come back and my presence of mind, my composure, would be destroyed.

As I said, we had a synagogue. An American army major, who was an ordained rabbi, served as a chaplain and took care of our religious needs and our comforts. In the beginning, I did not really attend services. I did not care. At that time, I had no feeling for it. I didn't miss it. The rabbi's main function was limited to performing weddings, of which there were quite a few, and things like counseling and advice. The chaplain never talked to us about the war, and I never talked to him about it. He did not want to deal with the past, with what had happened, because there were too many scars and too many reminders. He did not want to upset us. We just did not talk about it, and I didn't *want* to talk about it, either. I didn't want to open any wounds. This chaplain, unfortunately, was later killed in a car accident.

At first, I did not observe any kashrut at Bindermichel, although the food was kosher. Some of the Jews who arrived in the camp from other parts of Europe were *shochetim* (kosher slaughterers), so obtaining kosher meat was no problem for the administrators. In the beginning, I did not observe Jewish laws at all. It was sort of loose. I did not want to live with obligations. I sometimes went on Saturdays to daven, but only sometimes.

A typical day in Bindermichel was as follows. Life was very simple. I slept for as long as I wanted. I went to the kitchen for food, and then I just wandered around. We congregated. Someone established a restaurant in one of the barracks, and we would go there. We began to talk and to reminisce about Poland before the war—whenever Jews congregate, there's always something to talk about. We also talked about politics. Later on, I took up photography. I wasn't bored. Whoever wanted to work could get a job. I did not want to do any physical work, so I

Abe in front of the displaced persons camp, Bindermichel, 1946

The American chaplain at Bindermichel

didn't do any. There were theatrical performances. The administrators, along with the people in the camp, established an orchestra, and I went to the concerts. I enjoyed the concerts. They also had dances, and I attended the dances, just to keep myself entertained. If you wanted to do all these things, you could, because Bindermichel was like a city. There were always people coming and going. After all the horror I had gone through, life became easier.

A driving school was established, and I attended it. You could also go into town and see a movie, which my friends and I did. I saw movies like *Singing in the Rain* and *On the Town* with Frank Sinatra and Gene Kelly. I also went to see the *News of the World* newsreel, which was shown on Fridays. Sometimes they showed some Jewish movies in camp, movies with Molly Picon and Moishe Oysher, who was one of the greatest cantors in the world. I also remember hearing a *hazzan* (cantor), perform the *kiddush,* the prayer at the entrance of the Sabbath, over the radio. It always thrilled me to hear a Jewish voice coming over the radio. It must have been from the American Armed Forces Network. To this day I remain fascinated by *chazzones* (cantorial music).

The Zionist Organization was very active in Bindermichel. Another group, ORT, established sewing circles for women and groups to teach women all types of trades. The UNRRA, HIAS, and the JDC were in charge of the camp. They even established a Jewish police force to maintain order. They were not armed, but they kept order. There were also groups that provided help if you wanted to go to Palestine. You could register to go to Palestine. A lot of people went to Palestine from Bindermichel.

Every day, more and more people came to Bindermichel DP camp. A lot of Polish Jews arrived from Russia. Russia released them because they were Polish citizens. One day, to my surprise, I met my aunt, my uncle, and their children. This aunt was my father's sister. They were on their way from Russia through

Austria and Italy to Palestine. My aunt and uncle told me that they had survived only because Russia occupied the part of Poland where they were living, and the Russians sent them off to Siberia. My aunt and uncle had been sent by the Joint Distribution Committee, a refugee aid organization, to stay in a camp nearby called Wegshid. They were probably looking for family members when they arrived. Some other people let them know that there was a Zuckerman at Bindermichel, and that's how we met. Our meeting was very dramatic and very warm.

My aunt and uncle wanted to know about other family members, but, unfortunately, I had no good news for them. About six months later, they went on to Italy and then they finally reached Israel. They lived out the rest of their lives in Israel. Their children are still there, and I see them every time I go to Israel. I also knew that my mother had a sister in England, named Eva Lipshitz, so I knew I had some family there. My mother had told me that her sister had fled from her home in Austria to England when Hitler invaded Austria. I guess times weren't too great in Austria for her, because we used to send her food packages. While I was in Bindermichel, I wrote to the Red Cross for information about my aunt. One day, I received her address from the Red Cross. I kept in touch with her. My aunt even sent me food packages from London, but it wasn't really necessary because I did not go hungry in the camp.

At Bindermichel, my uncle gave me a pair of tefillin that he brought with him from Russia. Tefillin are the leather straps and boxes containing important quotations from the Bible. A Jewish male needs to wear tefillin in order to pray on weekday mornings. Somehow, this pair of tefillin made me go back to praying. Throughout most of my ordeal in the concentration camps, I had been able to keep with me the tefillin I received at my Bar Mitzvah. I cherished my tefillin although I didn't do any *davening* (praying) with them. I tried to keep them with me throughout all of my journeys from camp to camp. I was still a believer. I figured that my tefillin were something that should be with me.

I lost my Bar Mitzvah tefillin on my arrival at Mauthausen camp. We were all lined up and then marched naked to the showers, and we had to leave all our personal belongings in the street. When we came back from the showers, stark naked, the street was clean and everything, including my tefillin, had been taken away. I guess the pair of tefillin my uncle gave me at Bindermichel DP camp made me start to think about the way I was brought up. I knew that Jewish tradition was beautiful, and I guess I wanted to continue it. I suppose my uncle gave me my start in my return to *Yiddishkeit,* to Jewish practice.

Another survivor of the death camps who arrived in Bindermichel happened to have been a rabbi in the Polish town of Przemysl before the war, Rabbi Aharon Weitzner, shlita (may he live long and happily, amen). He became the chief rabbi of Bindermichel, and he did all of the necessities pertaining to Judaism for the population in the DP camp. He was very understanding of the situation of the people in the DP camp. He understood what we had experienced. You cannot expect that one who had witnessed the atrocities of the Holocaust would return immediately to Yiddishkeit once he had been liberated. Rabbi Weitzner believed that time would bring us back to Judaism. He was a survivor himself, and he knew what we were all going through. He believed that we would all come around someday, that our attachment to Yiddishkeit would be restored. I admired his courage for what he did then and what he is doing today. He was and is a wonderful person. Now he resides in Borough Park, in Brooklyn, and I am in touch with him to this day.

I mentioned that while I was in Julag, I encountered my cousin, Maximilian Hornung. We met once again in Bindermichel.

My cousin wanted to go back to Poland to resume his law practice. He also tried to find members of our family, but he had

Rabbi Aharon Zevi Weitzner, *shlita,* in 1947

Rabbi Aharon Zevi Weitzner performing wedding ceremony for Abe and Millie in Bindermichel, 1947

no more luck than I did. He returned to Poland, but tragically, he was killed in a car accident in 1946.

Soon after we were moved to Bindermichel, I was wondering what had happened to my friend Moniek Pantirer, as I had lost contact with him when I was moved from Plaszuw Camp. I tried to find out through different people what had happened to him. One day he showed up at the DP camp in Bindermichel; he was assigned to the same apartment building where I lived. We spent approximately four years together there. While in Bindermichel, Moniek and I both got married.

Fate led us to be together in America, too. Moniek emigrated to America about six months before I did, and when I arrived I inquired as to his whereabouts. We were reunited and we planned together how to start a new life for ourselves and our families. Moniek had taken a job at a butcher shop in the Bronx and I worked in a ladies clothing factory in Newark. We would often meet and debate our future and what type of business venture to go into. In August of 1950, Moniek and I, along with Moniek's uncle, the late Isak Levenstein, a fellow survivor, ventured into the building business in New Jersey. Moniek and I have been together as friends and business partners for forty years. *Ad meah v'esrim!* (Till a hundred and twenty!)

AUGUST, 1945: MY TRIP TO POLAND

WHILE I WAS IN BINDERMICHEL, I wanted very much to go to America, but first I wanted to see if I could find any remaining members of my family. I was very busy trying to find relatives while I was at Bindermichel. I decided one day that I myself should travel to Cracow to see if any of my relatives had survived. It was a difficult decision for me to go back to Cracow. I always thought that perhaps some of of my family would still be alive. I never believed that my parents were gone, that my family was dead. I never believed that the Nazis had murdered everyone in my family. I guess I had to go to my town in Poland to prove it to myself. I needed to go to Poland to give myself the peace of mind that would only come from knowing I had done everything I could to find my family. I couldn't rest. Before I went to America, I knew I had to make this trip.

I persuaded my friend Yekel Fuhrer, who was now in the DP camp with me, to come along. His parents had lived in the same house as my parents in Dukla. We undertook the journey to Cracow together. Some tailors in the DP camp made us suits out of some American blankets, and that's how we got dressed to go to Poland. It took us a few days to get there, because the war had just ended and there were no direct railroad connections. Many of the train tracks had been bombed. We hitchhiked, we traveled by trucks and trains, until we finally reached Cracow.

A friend of mine in Bindermichel had given me the name of a relative of his, a Jewish man who was an officer in the Polish army. This officer was stationed at the time in Cracow. Yekel and I went to see him, and we stayed in his house for the duration of our visit, which lasted only two days. He went everywhere with us. He protected us, because we feared for our lives to be in Poland then. Later, it turned out that we had been right to be afraid and to seek protection. We heard that a pogrom was staged in the Polish city of Kielce right after the war. About forty-two Jews were killed there.

When I arrived in Cracow, it seemed that nothing had changed since I had left. Cracow looked the same as when I had left it. However, all the apartments where the Jews had lived were now occupied by Poles. I was really afraid to go by myself to the house where I grew up. I feared that I might get killed or beaten up if I went into the house. The officer I mentioned came in with us—he really protected us.

When I went to my old house, I saw that the superintendent was living in our old apartment. I asked him if anyone from my family had come back, if anyone had come to the house, any relatives looking for me. He said nobody had come back. All his answers were negative. I was really sad, and he seemed indifferent to what I was feeling. That was the end of my visit to my old apartment building.

I also went to my aunts' and my uncles' apartments. Nothing. Not a soul was left. The same thing happened to Yekel Furer—he also found no one. The Jewish-owned stores, unfortunately, were all closed up. Some of them were boarded up. I went to the *Yiddishe Gemeinde,* the Jewish Community building, and I saw a lot of people there, but I didn't meet anyone I knew. The only

A 1988 photo of Abe and Millie in front of the entrance to the apartment where Abe lived, Krakowska no. 24

Abe and Millie in front of City Hall *(Ratusz)*, Wolnica Street, Cracow, 1987

thing I saw there was that the walls were covered with names of people searching for relatives and friends.

The purpose of my trip to Cracow was to convince myself that my family was not there, that they had not come back. I also wanted to leave word that I had come in search of them. I told the superintendent to tell anyone who might come to look for me that I was in Linz, Austria, at the DP camp in Bindermichel. I did not go to see anything else in Cracow. I was not interested. The atmosphere in Cracow was not very pleasant. We did not feel comfortable there, without our families and our friends—and without Jews. We saw very few Jewish people in Cracow. We knew we were better off in Bindermichel.

My friend Yekel and I picked ourselves up again. We had no luggage, nothing. We went back to the train station with our friend, the Jewish soldier, to make sure we got back safely on the train. Somehow, we went back to Austria and Bindermichel. We were happy to be back in Bindermichel. Looking back now, I realize how foolish it was at that time to have risked my life by traveling to Cracow. I was afraid of the Poles, but it was the same story as when Hitler first came to power—we minimized the danger. We pretended that the danger wasn't really there. Yekel and I didn't realize that we were risking our lives to look for relatives and visit our old homes.

MEETING MILLIE

FOR THE FIRST YEAR OR SO, I HAD NO desire to leave Bindermichel, because life was just starting to happen for me there. I was young and without a worry—I was still in the recuperation stage. My wounds were fresh. It took me about a year to wake up to the reality that there was a world outside of Bindermichel, that you had to think about the future, that you had to think about making a life for yourself and think about getting married.

Although there were far more young men than young women at Bindermichel, a lot of couples did meet—boy met girl, and they got married. After about a year, my attitude toward life began to change. The life I was leading hadn't changed, and I still lived in the same place, but finally I realized that this situation was temporary. I had to make a life for myself. It was then that I began to court my beautiful wife, and slowly we fell in love.

There weren't too many whole families at Bindermichel. As a matter of fact, out of thousands of people in the camp, there were only two or three families who had survived Hitler intact. By "intact" I mean that the parents and children had all managed to survive. Millie, her parents, and her sister were one of the families who had survived Hitler's atrocities. They survived only because they were hidden by Polish people. The young men in the camp, myself included, were all yearning to see what a whole family

Abe and Millie in Bindermichel

looked like, and the boys started to come to visit Millie and her family.

At Bindermichel, I started to visit Millie, and we fell in love. About a year after we met, her father suggested that we should get married. We both wanted to marry each other, and so we did. Rabbi Aharon Weitzner, the chief rabbi of Bindermichel, performed the ceremony. The wedding was in my room, and it was a very beautiful wedding with all our friends joining us.

We set up house in my room, which meant that the friend of mine who was rooming with me at the time had to leave and find different quarters.

One day, there was an announcement that President Harry Truman of the United States had signed a doctrine to admit 200,000 refugees to the United States. Millie and I, along with Millie's family, decided that we wanted to go there. UNRRA and

Abe and Millie on their wedding day, 1947

HIAS established a registration office for people who wanted to go to the United States. There was a lot of demand from around the world for the people who were in Bindermichel. Jewish organizations and private families in other countries wanted to sponsor the young people of Bindermichel and help them find a new life in a different country. For instance, somebody sent me sponsorship papers from Panama. I did not know who it was, but it must have been a Jewish family in Panama who wanted to sponsor me to go there. However, Millie and I decided to leave our memories behind and start a new life in the United States.

We registered and we had to go through all kinds of medical check-ups and paperwork. It took quite some time before we received permission to go to America. To be honest, I was not in a hurry to leave the camp. It was a comfortable life, and I did not know what to expect in America. I had no relatives there, so I was

New Year's greetings, first year of the liberation, 1946

Below: New Year's greetings a year later

Abe, standing in Honor Guard, at the First Anniversary Liberation Monument. A ceremony in Bindermichel, May 5, 1946

Yiddish inscription on the Liberation Monument reads: "To the Unknown Jewish Concentration Camp Prisoner, on the First Anniversary of Liberation, the Remembrance. May 5, 1946"

a little apprehensive. By then, Millie's parents were already in America. When word came that we could go to America, Millie and I were expecting our first child. Millie was in her seventh or eighth month, and they wouldn't let her travel by boat. Two months after our daughter Ann was born, we were notified that we could go to the United States. We were told that we were to travel by air, and that's how we went. We went first from Bindermichel by train to Munich, where we waited in a transit camp for a couple of months before we got the word that we could leave for the United States.

While we were in Munich, I went to meet that wonderful person who had been so kind to me in Dukla, Mr. Fritz Zachmann. I remembered his address from the first time he gave it to me, in the camp in Dukla. I never had to write it down. Kalbauchstrasse 80. I visited him, and then he came every day to the transit camp to see our baby and to play with her. It was very cordial and we were all happy that we could meet again in such wonderful circumstances.

I felt sad, though, to have left behind all my friends at Bindermichel, and now I was coming to a foreign land. In the beginning it was very strange for me. I came from Cracow, Poland, and now, after six years of internment and four years in the DP camp, I was coming to this enormous country, the United States. I was sad. All different kinds of emotions went through my head. It was very tough to leave behind the world I had known as a boy in Cracow. It was a very complicated emotion for me, for a while.

When I came to America, I resumed my Jewish tradition, Jewish law, and everything pertaining to it. I registered my daughter Ann when she was of age, in the Hebrew Academy of Newark. This may seem really striking. Many people would find it hard to understand that in spite of all I went through in the camps, I went back to *Yiddishkeit,* traditional Judaism. It is hard to explain, but when you are raised in the Jewish way of life, it is

First picture on arrival at Idlewild Airport in New York, May 29, 1949. *From left to right:* Abraham Mark, Millie's father; Isadore and Pearl Green, Millie's uncle and aunt; Freida Green, Millie's aunt; Millie with daughter, Ann; Mildred Burr, Millie's first cousin; and Millie's mother, Sabina Mark

Abe presenting a flower to his Aunt Pearl at his 60th birthday party

such a beautiful way of life that you cannot shake it off or deny it to yourself or to your children. I find Jewish tradition and the Jewish way of life beautiful. The Jewish tradition was very beautiful for me when I was growing up in Cracow. I believed that the Jewish tradition helps keep families together, and I wanted to keep my family together. You observe holidays together, you do things as a family. It's the most wonderful way to raise a family, as far as I'm concerned.

When we arrived in America, we were fortunate because Millie's mother had three sisters here.

The sisters and their husbands and some of their children waited for us at the airport when we arrived. One of the sisters, our aunt Pearl Green, with her husband, our uncle Izzie, took us into their home. Aunt Pearl had already taken my in-laws into her home when they came six months earlier. Aunt Pearl and Uncle Izzie had a medium-sized apartment which could not accommodate all these people. Then, when we came with the baby, she sent off her two children, Mildred and Billy, to sleep at the house of another member of her family, and Aunt Pearl gave us a room in which to sleep. That was very generous of her. Aunt Pearl was an exceptional woman. We did not stay very long there. After a week or so, we moved into our own apartment in Newark, New Jersey. We shared this apartment with Millie's parents.

A lot of my friends had no place to go when they arrived in the United States, so they were accommodated by the HIAS. In the beginning, shortly after our arrival, we congregated at the HIAS office on Lafayette Street in Manhattan. I went there often because I wanted to see who had arrived in the United States. I used to talk with the people who also went down there, and I always wanted to see if any of my friends had arrived. I was very lonely in the beginning, because I came from a little place, Bindermichel, where everything was taken care of for us. Now I had come to a country with a very different way of life. I was overwhelmed because there was everything under the sun in this country. To me it was unbelievable.

Immediately I knew that I had arrived in a free country. I could see and feel the freedom here and that you have the opportunity to accomplish whatever you desire. I was surprised that I did not need identification papers when I walked the streets. You could do things as free as you please. It is so true that America is the land of the free. This is the greatest country in the world, and I am proud that I chose it for my new home.

As for my parents and sisters, I never did learn of their fate. All I know is that they never came back. While I was in the concentration camps, I always thought that perhaps someone somehow would survive. I thought that someone might come back. But no one from my family ever returned.

Conclusion

MORE THAN FORTY YEARS HAVE PASSED since I was liberated from the concentration camps. To this day, I still think about the experience, about what I went through. The thoughts never go away and never will. Whenever I meet other survivors, no matter what else we talk about, the subject of our past experiences always comes up. I really don't believe it myself, that I went through these ordeals. I have only been able to tell you a little bit of the magnitude of the horrors that I survived.

It has not been easy for me to describe the events contained in this book. Anyone who was in the camps suffered enormously. We suffered because of the physical conditions—what we ate, what we could wear, how we were forced to live. We suffered because of the deprivations—we had lost our freedom, our right to live in dignity, our privacy, our security. We lived with the fear that our death might come at any moment. When that death came, we knew it would be a horrible and ignominious death, and that our bodies would be shoved into piles, burned in crematoria, or dumped into open trenches. We lived without dignity and we constantly expected to die without dignity. But the greatest, most horrible thing of all was that we knew our family members were also being tortured and killed. We could not help them and they could not help us. This feeling of utter helplessness and powerlessness is one that many Holocaust survivors can never forget and can never overcome.

The Holocaust is impossible for people to thoroughly understand. So much hate, so much violence, so much pain, and so much death for so many years—who could possibly grasp all this? When we hear large numbers—fifteen hundred people shot in a forest, two thousand people gassed to death—the mind reels. Something inside of us keeps us from feeling the full force of the horror of so many people dying at the same time. That six million Jews died and countless others suffered and were lucky enough to survive is practically inconceivable. And yet it happened. As it is the responsibility of my generation to tell the story of what we endured, so it is the responsibility of future generations to remember what happened, to try to understand it, and to do everything they possibly can to keep something like this from happening again.

As I told this story, I tried to concentrate on the details of my day-to-day life in the camps—what I ate, how I slept, what I wore, what work I was obligated to perform. By providing you with these facts, I am trying to let you understand exactly what my teenage years were like and how it felt to be a prisoner in these Nazi concentration and death camps. Much of the reading has been grisly but I have not tried to spare you from the facts. If you come away from these pages with a clearer picture of what life was like for the prisoners of the Nazis, then I have done my job.

Until I began to put my memories in writing, I never expected to delve this deeply into these experiences. Writing this book has caused me to think back on many sad occurrences in my life—above all, the time my parents were taken away from me, the last time I ever saw them alive. I think it might have been easier for me never to have revisited these extremely painful memories. But I could not bear the idea that my children and grandchildren and their children would never know what I had endured. I did not write this book only for them. I wrote it for everyone, to add my testimony to that of the people who have already written and spoken about their experiences in the camps. I had to add my voice to the chorus. As difficult as it has been to return in my mind to my childhood and to the camps, I am very glad that I have done so.

Humanity should learn from the Holocaust first and foremost that there is no place for religious or racial prejudice. Humanity should learn that when some crazy person gets up and starts to preach hatred or prejudice or violence, we should not take it lightly. We should not think that he's just a crazy person and that he'll just go away. This is simply wishful thinking. People in Europe said that Hitler was crazy, that he was a housepainter, and what does he know. And look what he did to the world. We should take these kinds of threats very seriously and try to stop them right away, not to wait. Another lesson of the Holocaust is that you shouldn't be fooled into thinking that something as horrible as this cannot happen.

How did I survive? It was not heroism that saved me. It just so happened that the war ended and I was lucky enough not to have been killed. As far as I am concerned, there were no heroes, really. The escapees were only the people who ran away from camp or people who jumped out of the little windows of the railroad freight cars when we were moved from camp to camp—and God knows what happened to them. There were a few resistance movements, like the Warsaw Ghetto, and in a few other places. But in the camps where I was interned, there were no heroes. There were no opportunities for heroism. We were doomed from day one, from the day we were placed in those camps. They were extermination camps. They were there just to humiliate you, to destroy you, to eliminate you.

In the beginning, when I was younger, I did not think back

on my experiences the way I do today. I guess when you are young, you are busy raising a family and your thinking focuses on your spouse and your children. You try to eliminate the past from your thoughts. When you get older it hurts more, but in the beginning I didn't look back. I was preoccupied with other things back then. I did not cry. It is hard, though. You try to tell your children why they don't have a grandfather or a grandmother or uncles or aunts or other family members. As my children grew up and I got a little older, I began to ask the question "Why?" Why did it happen? And why was I so lucky as to survive? The answer is luck. There's nothing else but luck and fate to explain it.

Today, whenever I think about my experiences during the war—the horrors that I went through—I lose my composure. It's very hard on me. The horrors are always on my mind, but when I don't talk about them, I feel pretty good. Anytime I get together with my friends, there isn't a conversation or even a moment that goes by when we do not discuss the horrible times. These horrors will never leave me. I hope that my story has helped you to understand what it was like to live through the Holocaust.

PART THREE

How MILLIE ZUCKERMAN AND HER FAMILY SURVIVED

THE STORY OF HOW MY WIFE, MILLIE, and her sister and her parents survived the Holocaust is an amazing one, and it deserves to be recorded in detail.

My wife, Millie, survived the Holocaust through the courage of her parents and the selflessness of a Polish woman named Michalina Kedra. Millie and her parents had been living until 1942 in a small Polish village called Humniska. This village was home to about five hundred families, of whom only twenty or so were Jewish. Millie's father ran a grocery store and so came to know and be known by the Polish people of the village. Millie attended public school in the village and grew up with Jewish and non-Jewish friends. When she was in elementary school, her parents hired a tutor to come to the house and teach her how to read, write, and pray in Hebrew. Millie says that she was conscious that her Jewishness made her seem different in the eyes of the other girls, but there were no overtly anti-Semitic acts.

Things changed, of course, when the war began in 1939. For the next three years, Millie and her family were permitted to remain in their home in Humniska, but they were obligated to wear armbands that identified them as Jews. Millie remembers this as a humiliating experience for her and her family. Her education was halted when she, her older sister, and her father were required from 1939 to 1942 to perform forced labor for the Nazis. Somehow the Nazis did not obligate older women to perform hard labor. Millie, her sister, and her father were transported by bus six mornings a week at eight o'clock to the worksite, where they were forced to carry stones that were used as paving stones for roads.

The times were very hard for everyone, but especially for young people, because there was no education and no entertainment like movies. There was only the forced labor. Millie says she thought it would last forever, but her parents always said that it couldn't possibly last forever. The attitude of most Jews in the town was that the war could only last another week or two at most, and then they would be rid of the Nazis. They never imagined that the Nazi occupation of Poland would last five years. The Jews of Millie's town even heard reports of the liquidations of Jews elsewhere in Europe, but somehow no one could believe those reports. People believed that although these atrocities were happening elsewhere, they could never happen in Humniska.

In 1942, things changed for the worse. Millie's father was no longer able to keep his grocery open. The family lived for some months on his savings. And then the Nazis decided to make the entire area surrounding Humniska *Judenfrei*—free of Jews. Millie and her family, along with the other Jewish families of the town, were arrested by the Nazis and were moved to a neighboring, slightly larger village, Brzozuw. There, they were forced to do work like street paving and other forms of hard labor. The Jews of Brzozuw were forced to live packed together in schoolhouses.

After a short period, the Jews were moved to another town and another schoolhouse. And after a week or two working in that other town, the Jews were moved back to Brzozuw.

Several days after the return to Brzozuw, on a Sunday in September, 1942, the order came down from the Nazis that all the Jews were to assemble the next day in a stadium across from the town church. They were told to bring a small amount of clothing because they would be provided with clothing where they were going. Of course, by this time, Millie, her family, and the rest of the Jews in Brzozuw only had a limited amount of clothing. The Nazis told the Jews that they would be going to a labor camp, where they would be able to earn a living. Millie's father resolved not to go. He sensed that the Jews of Brzozuw would not be transported somewhere. He sensed that they all would be murdered. He wanted the family to try to escape.

Millie's mother was extremely unhappy about the idea of escaping. Her mother and sister lived in Brzozuw, and she could not abide the idea of being separated from them. Millie's mother and sister did not want to leave Brzozuw and try to escape. In the end, though, Millie's father prevailed. That night, instead of preparing to go the stadium the next day, Millie, her sister, and her parents escaped Brzozuw together and went back to their hometown of Humniska. They had little clothing, little money, and no idea of where to go. Humniska was supposed to be *Judenfrei* by now—free of Jews.

Millie's father decided to seek refuge at the home of a Polish friend, a widow with four children, Michalina Kedra. Mrs. Kedra was a longtime customer of Millie's father's grocery store. Millie and Mrs. Kedra's daughter Helena, moreover, were friends from school. At times when Mrs. Kedra could not afford to pay her grocery bills, Millie's father would extend her credit, saying that Mrs. Kedra's children had to eat. Mrs. Kedra never forgot this kindness, and she once told Millie's father that if he ever needed help because of the Nazi occupation, he should come to her.

Michalina Kedra (b. August 9, 1905; d. June 16, 1968). Millie will always remember and pay special tribute to Michalina Kedra, the righteous Gentile who saved the lives of Millie, her mother, father, and sister, at great personal sacrifice and for no reward except the knowledge that she was doing the right thing.

The Kedra home, Humniska, Poland, where Millie and her family hid during the war

So, under cover of darkness, Millie and her family arrived at Mrs. Kedra's door, and asked if she could hide them for a day or two, until they could determine what to do next. Now, any Pole caught sheltering Jews would be put to death immediately. And Mrs. Kedra and her common-law husband, who lived with her, had four children of their own to feed in a very small house. Nevertheless, the Kedra family agreed to hide Millie, her sister, and her parents. The next day, Mrs. Kedra told Millie's father that he was lucky. At the stadium, just as Millie's father had predicted, the Nazis took the fifteen hundred or more Jews who had appeared as ordered, marched them to a forest, and executed them. The entire Jewish population of the area had been liquidated.

Millie's family was in tears when they heard this news, because they assumed—correctly—that Millie's grandmother, aunt, and all their other relatives had been shot to death in the liquidation at Brzuzow. For the next two years, Millie and her family lived in the attic and stable of Mrs. Kedra's house.

One time, the Nazis came and Millie's family slipped behind the false wall. Unfortunately, they had left in plain sight a chamberpot and Millie's father's watch. Somehow, through the grace of God, the Nazi soldiers who noticed these things did not say anything about them to anyone. The lives of the Kedra family and of Millie's family were spared.

Living this way was extremely lonely and difficult for Millie and her family. Years later, Millie said that she could not remember how they passed the time from hour to hour. Mrs. Kedra's daughter often visited Millie, and they would spend the time talking. As I said, Millie's family lived this way for two whole years.

Millie's family was finally liberated by the Russians in August, 1944. The Russians beat back the Nazis in Poland, but during the battles, the town of Humniska found itself in no-man's-land. The Kedras, along with all the other residents of the town, were forced to abandon their home. Of course, Millie's family had to stay behind. Millie's family had to survive four or five days of bombardment by the Russian and German artillery. They had no food. Finally Mrs. Kedra crossed the Russian lines—against the orders of the Russian officers—to bring food to Millie's family. "Now you're going to be free," Mrs. Kedra told them. Millie remembers that she could barely swallow the food because they had gone so long without eating.

Finally, the bombardment ended and Millie's family, along with half a dozen other Jews who had also been hidden by Polish families, were liberated. Their liberators were ten Russian soldiers on horseback. Freedom for Millie's family brought mixed emotions. They were glad to be out of the attic, but they had to cope with the fact that no one else from their families, or even the entire area, had survived.

The barn and trapdoor in the attic where Millie and her family hid for two years

Millie and Helena Bocon during a recent visit in America. Helena is the daughter of Michalina Kedra.

Abe and Millie planting a tree for Michalina Kedra (b. August 9, 1905, d. June 16, 1968), Avenue of the Righteous, Yad Vashem, Jerusalem

Millie and I are still close with Mrs. Kedra's daughter, Helena Bocon, and we have visited each other here in the United States and in Poland. We saw to it that the Kedras were honored by Yad Vashem for their unbelievably courageous actions. A tree has been planted along the Avenue of the Righteous at Yad Vashem in their honor. Yad Vashem was established by the Israeli Martyrs and Heroes Remembrance Act of 1953 as a memorial to those who perished in the Holocaust. Yad Vashem was named from a verse of Isaiah in which God makes the following promise:

> I will give [to them] in my house and within my walls
> a place and a name
> better than sons or daughters.
> I will give them an everlasting name which
>   shall not be cut off.

Thanks to the extraordinary kindness of Michalina Kedra, Millie and her family survived the Holocaust intact.

A recent photo of Abe Zuckerman and his wife, Millie

Opposite: The plaque in honor of Michalina Kedra at Yad Vashem

My aunts and uncles who perished in the Holocaust

FROM MY FATHER'S SIDE	FROM MY MOTHER'S SIDE
Zanwul Zuckerman	Nathan Hornung
Chaim Zuckerman	Sara Gross
Akiwa Zuckerman	Pola Lupschutz*
Leib Zuckerman	Gitcia Wiener
Pesil Zuckerman	Leha Hornung
Dina Beer*	Ann Zuckerman
Rioza Mandel	Jula Grossfeld
Beila Green	*Died of natural causes

Their deaths and the deaths of all who perished in the Holocaust are a reminder that we must never forget what did happen and that we must always remember what can happen. May their souls rest in peace.

Streets Named for Herr Oskar Schindler

The following is a list of towns in New Jersey and Pennsylvania in which streets have been named for Oskar Schindler, the man who saved the lives of Abraham Zuckerman, Murray Pantirer and countless other Jews during the Holocaust.

Borough of South Plainfield
Borough of New Providence
Township of Berkeley Heights
Township of Old Bridge
Township of Bridgewater
Township of East Brunswick
Township of Roxbury
Township of Brick
Township of Rockaway
Township of Randolph
Township of Long Hill
Borough of Chatham
Township of Hanover
Township of Washington
Township of Clark
Township of Livingston
Township of West Orange
Schindler Plaza, Union
Township of Hillside
Township of Lower Makefield, Pennsylvania
Township of Fairfield
Borough of Florham Park
Township of Bernards
Township of Neptune
Borough of Upper Saddle River

About the Author

Abraham Zuckerman, a Holocaust survivor, was born in Cracow, Poland. He emigrated to the United States in 1949 and has been in the real estate business for the past forty years. He is a member of the board of American Gathering of Holocaust Survivors, a founding member of the Simon Wiesenthal Center for Holocaust Studies, a trustee of the New York Holocaust Heritage Museum, a fellow of Yad Vashem in Jerusalem, and a founding member of the Holocaust Memorial Museum in Washington, D.C.

Mr. Zuckerman is also a member of the Executive Committee of the Holocaust Research Center at Kean College; President of the Jewish Education Center of Elizabeth, New Jersey; and a Builder of the Hiydra Rabba Yeshiva of Jerusalem. He is a supporter of the Jerusalem Foundation; the New Cracow Society; and the Rabbinical College of America. He is also a member of the Board of Governors of the Great Synagogue of Jerusalem.

Mr. Zuckerman recently received a Doctor of Laws degree from the Rabbinical College of America.

In 1996, Mr. Zuckerman received an Honorary Doctorate of Law from Kean College of New Jersey.

Mr. Zuckerman and his wife, Millie, also a Holocaust survivor, have three children—Ann, Ruth, and Wayne, and eight grandchildren—Debbie, Jeffrey, Hillary, Michelle, Jennifer, Stephanie, Andrew and David. A Great granddaughter, Julia.

Mr. and Mrs. Zuckerman reside in Hillside, New Jersey.

The following photographs represent various aspects of Abraham Zuckerman's remarkable life after the Holocaust. From the despair and desolation of internment in seven concentration camps, Abraham not only survived, he rebuilt and renewed his life and his family. Yet he never forgets his past and always keeps the flame of remembrance eternally kindled. From presidents to world leaders, honorary degrees to street names in honor of Oskar Schindler, Abraham Zuckerman has become a successful real estate developer, community leader, noted philanthropist and loving grandfather and great-grandfather.

Meeting
Abe and Millie with the
First Prime Minister Of Israel
David Ben-Gurion
In Israel 1967

Abraham Zuckerman at age 12.

Abe and Millie with their Grandchildren
Clockwise:
David, Michelle, Jennifer, Jeffrey,
Stephanie, Hillary, Debbie and her husband, Neil,
Andrew and Millie holding Great Granddaughter, Julia

Abe presenting his book to
President Clinton

Abraham Zuckerman standing beside
A Street named in honor of
Oscar Schindler

Abe during the ceremony when he received
an Honorary Doctorate Degree
From Kean College in 1995
On his right are: Malcolm M. Forbes, Jr.
and The President of the College Elsa Gomez

Abe with his son, Wayne, On a visit to
K Z Mauthausen , Austria
Standing on the famous 186 steps leading
to The Quarry

Visiting the roots of our parents
In Poland
August 11, 1994

From Left: Deborah Zuckerman,
Abraham Zuckerman, Ann Sklar, Ruth Katz,
Millie Zuckerman

Attending the 50th Anniversary of the Liberation of Mauthausen in Austria
May 7, 1995 with his family
From Left: Wayne Zuckerman, Steven Katz
Bernard Sklar, Millie and Abe

Abe Presenting his book to
the President Of Israel, Chiam Herzog
and his wife Ora, In Israel -1991

Portrait of Abe used in the book
"The Triumphant Spirit"
By Nick Del Calzo
1997